Adulthood is often a mixture of crisis, turmoil, challenge, and growth. Dr. Gary R. Collins says that how well you move through adulthood depends on how you handle the changes in life. In the pages that follow, you'll find insight and advice for dealing with these and other areas of change:

- *adulthood*
- *independence*
- *marriage*
- *singleness*
- *parenthood*
- *spiritual maturity*
- *career building*

Getting Started will help you develop important life skills for getting well established in your adult years.

Getting Started

Direction for the most important decisions of life.

Gary R. Collins

Power Books

Fleming H. Revell Company
Old Tappan, New Jersey

Unless otherwise identified, Scripture quotations in this volume are from the HOLY BIBLE, NEW INTERNATIONAL VERSION. Copyright © 1978 by the New York International Bible Society. Used by permission of Zondervan Bible Publishers.

Scripture verses marked TLB are taken from *The Living Bible,* Copyright © 1971 by Tyndale House Publishers, Wheaton, Ill. Used by permission.

Scripture quotations identified NASB are from the New American Standard Bible, © The Lockman Foundation 1960, 1962, 1963, 1968, 1971, 1972, 1973, 1975, 1977.

Scripture quotations identified PHILLIPS are from THE NEW TESTAMENT IN MODERN ENGLISH, Revised Edition—J. B. Phillips, translator. © J. B. Phillips 1958, 1960, 1972. Used by permission of Macmillan Publishing Co., Inc.

Material from THE SEASONS OF A MAN'S LIFE, by Daniel J. Levinson et al. Copyright © 1978 by Daniel J. Levinson. Reprinted by permission of Alfred A. Knopf, Inc.

Quote from "A Hymn to Him" is Copyright © 1956 by Alan Jay Lerner and Frederick Loewe. Chappell & Co., Inc., owner of publication and allied rights throughout the world. International Copyright Secured. ALL RIGHTS RESERVED. Used by permission.

Excerpt from *Calm Down* by Gary R. Collins is © Copyright 1981, Vision House, Ventura, CA 93006. Used by permission.

Library of Congress Cataloging in Publication Data

Collins, Gary R.
    Getting started.

    "Power books."
    Includes bibliographical references.
    1. Young adults—Conduct of life.   I. Title.
BJ1661.C627   1984   248.8′4   84-6840
ISBN 0-8007-5162-0

Contents

Getting Started

The Challenge of Young Adulthood

1

Becoming an Adult

Handling Your Transition Into Adulthood

At last we were on our way. We had said our sad good-byes, the apartment key had been turned in, and our little, green Volkswagen bug, stuffed to overflowing with all of our worldly possessions, was taking us east, just as the sky ahead was beginning to show the flickering rays of a rising summer sun. Reluctantly, we were leaving the Pacific Northwest paradise where we had gone to school, fallen in love, and exchanged our marriage vows only four weeks earlier.

Moving to a different part of the country, starting new jobs, finding an apartment, locating a church, making new friends, nurturing an infant marriage—all of this was both exciting and scary to contemplate as we drove through the Rockies and across the long miles of prairies. When we reached the Minnesota community that was to be our home for four years, we settled in quickly, buoyed, I suspect, by youthful enthusiasm, ambitious idealism, and a boundless spirit of adventure. The little apartment we rented was in a brand-new building, but apart from the wall-to-wall carpet (which wasn't ours) and the debris unloaded from our Volkswagen, the rooms were starkly empty.

So off we went to garage sales and secondhand stores, where we found all kinds of precious items. We located an old kitchen table, three almost-stable chairs, and a chest of drawers that we bought for eight dollars, plus two dollars' delivery charge because we couldn't find any way to get furniture into or on top of our little car.

Far from our families, we soon found friends to enjoy and appreciate. These were friends who could encourage and help us in times of uncertainty. One understanding couple even loaned us a bed; and we discovered that people were more than willing to invite us over for coffee or in for an occasional free meal.

But as summer turned into fall and winter, we discovered that the warmth of the people was in radical contrast to the weather. I had grown up in Canada but even that hadn't prepared me for the arctic winds that blew down over the western prairies, picked up speed (and sometimes snow) as they rushed in our direction, and never stopped until they hit me in the face as I walked to work on those winter mornings. Once I got to work and thawed out, I found the job to be challenging. The students were stimulating and teaching was fun, but the academic load almost overwhelmed me, and my assistant professor's salary was incredibly low. Looking back we realize now that this first year of marriage was one of the most difficult times in our lives.

At the college where I taught, one of my responsibilities was to develop a course entitled Developmental Psychology. I had always assumed that development and growth were lifelong events, but Freud seemed to think otherwise, and so did many of the people who wrote the textbooks I surveyed in preparing my course. These writers said much about child psychology and adolescence but they left the impression that the challenging part of life is over by the time we turn eighteen. In the library there were books about student radicals and volumes that dealt with the problems of aging. Soon we would be bombarded with writings about middle age. But at that time, and to a large extent even now, the period of early adulthood was overlooked by psychologists and other writers. Had these authors forgotten the fun and frustrations of being a young adult?

As a beginning college teacher, not much older than my students, I couldn't forget the uncertainties that came with those early years of adulthood. I had a job, a good marriage, and a place to live, but I also had a host of insecurities and a lot of pressure to succeed. It is during our twenties and early thirties that we set the course for the rest of our time on earth. The die that shapes the future usually is cast long before we reach middle age. I knew that some of my contemporaries would "make it" in this life and others would not. Some of my former college classmates had already launched promising careers, but others were like D. S. Preston, a young free-lance writer who was honest enough to write about his frustrations in a thought-provoking magazine article.

"Who am I?" is not, I suppose, an uncommon question for someone in his late twenties to be asking himself. It is a time of crisis for many, as dreams born and nurtured in late teens and early twenties are seldom realized as fully as they were conceived. Dreams do die hard.

It has not been pleasant to realize that I have not achieved the success I once thought I and any college graduate could reasonably hope for. I now know that despite the myths our society endeavors to perpetuate, higher education no longer (if it ever did) guarantees employment or prestige.

The job market is tight to nonexistent in many fields, and one cannot realistically look for this to change. . . .

But what does a person do when, after years of study and hard work, his dreams of success never materialize in the ways he thought they should? What happens when the world around fails to confirm the image he has of himself?

For me, at least, I have questioned my worth as a person. Although I continue to apply for jobs across the country, I have been unable thus far to find one commensurate with either my skills or aspirations. I have not been told by the means most acceptable in our country—through the securing of a job and, ultimately, making a "decent salary"—that I really am as good as the diplomas on the wall indicate.

Diploma poor, and with no prospects in sight of financial relief or ego support, I have been forced to realize that my spiritual poverty is as great as, if not greater than, my financial poverty. The crisis of having to come to terms with myself and with society has caused me to realize the emptiness of the spiritual rhetoric I have used for years. . . .

One thing indicating my lack of living faith is the frantic anxiety that has come to dominate my life—the overconcern about what I shall eat and what I shall drink and what I shall wear. I have had to ask myself: Is this the normal state of a Christian?[1]

Life's Turning Points

The "normal state" for one person may not be normal for somebody else. Each of us is a unique collection of past experiences, hopes for the future, personality traits, innate abilities, and acquired learning. No two people make an identical pilgrimage through this life.

For each of us, however, life involves passage through a series of *transformations.*[2] The helpless infant is transformed into a toddler and later becomes a kindergartner. The twelve-year-old becomes a teenager and during the next few years is transformed into a high school graduate. The single young adult may be transformed into a marriage partner and later into the role of a young parent. All of these transformations are turning points—times of moving from one stage in life to another. Some of the transformations are easy, but many are not. Most involve uncertainty, readjustment, and an ability to cope with change.

When my wife and I moved during that first year of our marriage, we were undergoing a variety of transformations: from singleness to marriage, from student to faculty status, from dependence on families to greater independence. Such transformations are easier when we expect them, when they come one at a time, and when friends and family are available to help. It is harder to handle transformations we aren't expecting and can't control. This partially explains why divorce, the death of a child, or the sudden loss of health are so difficult. D. S. Preston had a forced transformation from involvement in an idealistic college setting where there was promise of a bright, successful future, into the realistic but discouraging ranks of the unemployed. This transformation was especially difficult because it was unwanted, unexpected, and apparently impossible to predict.

Almost all transformations involve at least some struggling. Such struggles are rarely pleasant, but without them we seldom grow, mature, or escape from boredom. The brother of Jesus hinted at this many centuries ago when he made the incredible statement that we should actually rejoice when trials come into life, since these struggles lead us to maturity (James 1:2–4).

All of life, then, is marked by change, stress, and a need to adjust to transformations. This is especially true of young adulthood, a time of life between the late teens and mid-thirties when most of us are getting established as fully grown members of the society in which we live. There can be a lot of frustration, discouragement, failure, and anger during these years; but this can also be a period of life when we are free to explore new worlds, to find new identities, to enjoy life, and to be creative. It is a time for enthusiasm, idealism, and hope. It also is a time when we are confronted with a variety of decisions and the "life tasks" that prepare us for later adulthood.

Life's Tasks

In 1950, a Harvard professor named Erik Erikson proposed that life can be divided into eight stages.[3] Each of these presents us with an important challenge; each involves a crisis which must be faced and resolved if we are to mature and grow into the next stage of life.

Erikson's first four stages deal with young children. Since we are more concerned with people who are older, let's look first at stage five. This is the time of adolescence, a period of life during which teenagers struggle with questions of identity: *Who am I? Where do I fit in this world? How do others see me? What do I believe and why? Where am I going?* These are not easy questions to answer, and many young people find themselves involved in what has been called an "identity crisis."[4] This is a time of turmoil as each individual struggles to decide what is right and wrong, how to get along with parents and friends, and how to fit into the adult world now that one has an adult body. The struggles at this time in life are (to use Erikson's term) struggles between "identity versus role confusion."

By the time we reach twenty most of us discover that we are moving into a new stage. Life seems less confused and we have clearer identities, but soon we begin a struggle between "intimacy versus self-absorption." Intimacy involves a lot more than sex. The intimate person could be better described as someone who is genuinely concerned about others, willing to give help and encouragement, and inclined to share. After a long struggle to find identity, the young adult is now ready and eager to fuse his or her identity with others and to make commitments.

At the same time, there is a tendency to be competitive, independent, withdrawn, and absorbed in ourselves. What is hard to understand is the fact that sometimes we withdraw from and compete with our most intimate friends. With the same people we show both the desire for intimacy and its opposite—the inclination to be absorbed in ourselves. The young couple, for example, may have periods of close tenderness interspersed with times of withdrawal conflict and self-centered independence. Business associates may vacillate between working together as a team and competing with each other for promotions or attention from the boss. Students may cooperate fully as lab partners, but compete for grades. Young adults may be torn between a desire to get along well with parents and the urge to break away in order to live on one's own while pursuing personal interests.

According to Erikson, this struggle between intimacy and self-absorption is the major task of young adulthood. In time, most of us are able to build intimate relationships with others and with God, but some people, even those who are married, allow themselves to remain in self-absorption. Lacking close friends and overly concerned about careers or personal problems, these people slip into loneliness and sometimes become very unhappy. Slowly they learn that a life focused primarily on oneself and on one's own interests often is a life of insecurity, boredom, and deep emptiness.

D. S. Preston, that unemployed writer whom we met earlier, has learned some important lessons about intimacy and the need to rise above self-absorption.

I have been forced to ask myself if I really believe in what the Lord's Prayer says: "Give us this day our daily bread." My answer has been no. I have been satisfied with neither the provisions for the day nor the day's provisions. If I had, the degree of anxiety I have experienced over lack of position and lack of recognition, and uncertainty about the future and the size of my salary would never have troubled me so, making me unhappy with myself and others.

Money, position, and prestige, then, are those things I have used to determine my value. My happiness and even my identity have been contingent upon what the world esteems. I have been unable to rest cheerfully in the now with what I have—or rather, with what I do not have.

In my disillusionment, I have learned that the really important question to ask is not who am I or what do I do or how much do I make. These are things I have had little control over so far and are of very little significance eternally. Rather, what is necessary for me, as a Christian, is to ask, Whose am I? To center one's person on the person of Christ, to pursue him rather than wealth and position, is to find value in this life and salvation in the next. It is to enter into an existence so wholly other than what most of us live, an existence in which the trains we must catch run on a different schedule and have different destinations than those of the world. It is an existence whose grammar is totally different from that spoken by the world. Who you work for or what you do become questions of little importance. Why you work at a certain job and how you perform that job are the important issues—issues the disenfranchised and disenchanted college graduate and Ph.D. will need to struggle with more and more.

It is a wonderfully freeing existence, which, in a very real sense, opens up job possibilities for the Christian. It is an existence in which ungodly, self-serving motives about career are crucified to the glory of God and to the benefit of one's fellows. And so I feel now that I need not go through life thinking of myself as a failure, bemoaning all my glorious unrealized potential which, should it ever be achieved, would most likely be spiritually detrimental.

The question is not, Who am I, but Whose am I?[5]

Later in life, most of us will come to a stage of "generativity versus stagnation." This is a time, in our forties and fifties, when we stagnate (while we wait for retirement and become progressively self-centered, materialistic, intellectually dull, and sometimes hypercritical), or move on to actively encourage and enthusiastically guide the next generation by our parenting, teaching, and involvement in changing the society. By the time we reach sixty and move into the last stage of life, our earlier choices will almost have determined how we deal with the conflict between "integrity versus despair." People who are characterized by integrity can lean back with a sense of satisfaction and a realistic appraisal of life. These individuals feel good about themselves and about the way life's challenges have been met. In contrast, there are other people who end life in despair—bitter, discouraged, and preoccupied with missed opportunities.

Have you ever pondered what you will be like if you survive into the later years? To some extent—although not entirely— your attitudes in old age will depend on life circumstances over which you have little control. But even when life is difficult we can develop a positive outlook and resist the tendency to complain and wallow in bitterness. To avoid stagnation in middle age or despair in the later years, it is important that we develop intimacy and more positive attitudes when we are younger. This is a major task of young adulthood.

Life's Transitions

In our society, when does a young person become an adult? That deceptively simple question is not easy to answer. Some people reach their full adult height at age twelve or thirteen, and the ability to function sexually as an adult comes even sooner. Those living in America can be tried as adults in a court of law at sixteen, but must be eighteen to vote and at least thirty before they are eligible to run for election to the United States Senate. People in their mid-twenties are still referred to as "college kids," even when they have marriages and mortgages, but teenage girls are often pushed to make "adult" decisions about issues such as contraception or abortion.

Unlike those societies that hold elaborate and clearly defined initiation ceremonies, we mark the coming of adulthood in vague and sometimes confusing ways. Surely there is truth in the observation that the twenties are, for most people, a time of apprenticeship and self-evaluation through which we move before taking our places as fully accepted and responsible adult members of society. Some people move through the apprenticeship quickly; others seem to remain immature and childish for their entire lives.

This conclusion was emphasized several years ago when a team of researchers at Yale University published the results of an in-depth study of young adulthood.[6] While they acknowledged the "enormous influence" of Erikson's work, these Yale professors suggested that Dr. Erikson was a "student of life more than an academic scientist." In contrast, the Yale researchers, working under the direction of a psychologist named Daniel J. Levinson, wanted to discover precisely what happens to people as they move through the "preparatory" or "novice" phase of adulthood—the period from age seventeen or eighteen until one is thirty-two or thirty-three. According to the scientific findings, entering adulthood is a "lengthy and complex process" during which most of us go through several transitions in the years between high school and the early forties.

I've noticed this in a friend who recently turned twenty. I'll call him Todd, although that's not his real name. We have known each other since he was in high school, working in a fast-food restaurant and complaining because he never had a chance to drive the family car.

During the past three years, Todd has bought his own car, spent a year or two at college, struggled with dating and interpersonal relationships, tried to build a smoother bond with his parents and younger sisters, questioned some of his spiritual values, vacillated between cold and lukewarm attitudes toward the church, and worked to develop career goals which, at least for now, seem clear. I've spent many hours with Todd, usually sipping coffee in restaurants and listening as he gripes, ponders issues out loud, dreams, and expresses "firm" opinions that sometimes change within a week.

Levinson's research would say that Todd is in the *early adult transition* period. This is a five-year period beginning around age seventeen. It is a time when we leave high school and make preliminary steps into the world of adults. For many people this involves moving out of the family home, becoming less dependent financially on parents, and finding new friends. Often there is an exploring of new interests, values, or beliefs. For most of us, there is "greater psychological distance from the family, and reduced emotional dependency on parental support and authority."[7] None of this is easy. Todd has shown me that there sometimes is conflict, sadness, insecurity, and even grief as one begins to let go of childhood forever. But there is also excitement, enthusiasm, and a naive idealism which clouds many of the realities of moving into an adult world.

Entering the adult world is the next of Levinson's transition stages. Between twenty-two or twenty-three and the late twenties, the young adult is involved in exploring options for the future and making at least some choices about issues such as occupational direction, marriage, and life-style.

What the Yale researchers write about men in this period could doubtless be applied to women as well. As you read the following, you may want to ponder the extent to which these paragraphs describe you.

The young man has two primary yet antithetical tasks: (a) He needs to *explore* the possibilities for adult living: to keep his options open, avoid strong commitments and maximize the alternatives. This task is reflected in a sense of adventure and wonderment, a wish to seek out all the treasures of the new world he is entering. (b) The contrasting task is to create a *stable life structure:* become more responsible and "make something of my life." Each task has sources and supports in the external world and in the self.

Finding a balance between these tasks is not an easy matter. If the first predominates, life has an extremely transient, rootless quality. If the second predominates, there is the danger of committing oneself prematurely to a structure, without sufficient exploration of alternatives. . . .

A man has until roughly age twenty-eight or twenty-nine to explore the possibilities of adult life and to fashion a first, provisional life structure. This structure has multiple facets: a pattern of relationships with women, usually leading to marriage and family; an involvement in work which leads to forming an occupation; a home base as bachelor or married person, in a particular kind of dwelling, neighborhood and larger community; a pattern of relationships with parents and family of origin; an involvement, great or small, in religious, political, recreational, and other groups. . . .

For most men, the life structure of the late twenties is unstable, incomplete and fragmented. A man may have had a series of jobs and yet have no occupation or clear occupational direction. Although a transient existence without heavy responsibilities may have suited him well for a while, the insecurity and rootlessness of this life begin to weigh on him. If he has not yet married, the question of marriage becomes more urgent and he begins to examine more closely his usual form of relationship with women, such as shy avoidance of real contact, sexual promiscuity, enduring but nonsexual friendships, or intense but abortive affairs. The lacks and limitations in his life structure become intolerable. It is more distressing now if he does not have a wife or an occupation or a home base of his own. He becomes more aware that his life has no center, that it is fragmented into parts he cannot integrate.[8]

When I read the above paragraphs to a group of young adults, I once was interrupted by a student who suggested that all of this makes life seem like a mine field through which we tiptoe gently, hoping to reach middle life unscathed. It is true, of course, that life involves much more than difficulties, contradictions, fragmentation, and confusion. But this does not deny the fact that we live in a complex world which isn't always fair, which expects us to make hard decisions, and which sometimes serves us with disappointments like those that D. S. Preston expressed so clearly.

It doesn't help when well-meaning parents and friends exert subtle (and not-so-subtle) pressure to grow up, get married, settle down, get established, or decide "what you're going to do with your life." Sometimes parents or teachers give labels, suggesting, for example, that you are "a promising young scientist," "a natural mother," or "a young man who will do well in the family business." These descriptions are difficult to ignore if one's interests or vocational goals are in a different direction. "Everybody in my church expects me to be a preacher," a young seminarian confided shortly before getting his degree in theology, "but nobody at home knows that I don't want to enter the ministry." It isn't easy to face the reality of conflicts like this.

Nevertheless, most of us eventually reach the *age thirty transition.* In the five years surrounding age thirty, we begin to realize that the training period is over. We have been "grown-up" for over ten years and now must answer questions like: *What am I doing with my life? Where have I been going? Are there things I want to change, exclude, or add to life? Is this how I want to live for the next thirty years? If I don't change soon, will it be too late?*

In response to these questions, we either alter the course of life or continue in the direction that was charted during our twenties. Even society, tolerant of change and vacillation in younger adults, now expects us to settle down and build a career, family, and place in the community.

For many, movement into their thirties is smooth and hardly noticed. Such people have found a satisfactory occupation, have good relationships with family and friends, have settled into a life-style, and see no need to make major changes.

According to Levinson's research, however, it is much more common to experience stress and turmoil as we approach thirty. Youthful idealism has faded and the real problems of adult living have become clearer. Reports of the "mid-life crisis" begin to sound familiar, and many young adults conclude that they are experiencing all of the mid-life turmoil ten years too soon.

I saw this recently in one of my students. He is thirty-two, bright, handsome, and close-to-panic about the future. Rick's first marriage failed and his second is floundering, to some extent because his wife is losing patience over his inability to settle into a career choice. After getting a college degree, he started law school but dropped out. He worked in sales for a while, then entered a master's program in business administration. After leaving that, he began work on a counseling degree, but now has decided that this doesn't interest him as a career. He suspects, probably correctly, that the counseling major was selected primarily to find solutions to his own problems. Rick is cynical, angry, and hypercritical. To quote the Yale researchers, Rick is one of many who has encountered "great difficulty in working on the developmental tasks of this period. The difficulty is so great that at times he feels he cannot go on.

It is as though he had no basis for further living. . . . He experiences the imminent danger of chaos, dissolution, the loss of a future."[9] Saddest of all, perhaps, is that Rick doesn't want to let his Christianity help him at all.

It is difficult to predict what might happen to Rick. Although this doesn't always happen, some researchers suggest that people who are floundering at thirty-two or thirty-three, tend to flounder for the rest of their lives.

More common is the move into a *settling down* period which takes us through the remainder of our thirties. No longer novice adults, each of us works both to establish a place in society and to attain some measure of success and advancement. Life at this time is like climbing a ladder toward success. At the top there may be status, money, influence, a good family life, the possibility of making significant social contributions, creative achievement, business accomplishments, and increasing personal and spiritual maturity. There is evidence that for many people, the greatest period of creativity and discovery occurs in these years before forty.[10]

Like the periods that come before, this time in life also has its share of problems. Many people find, for example, that they are torn between a desire to be affirmed or applauded by society, and a wish to be independent and free from rat-race pressure. Perhaps most of us try to walk between these alternatives. We work hard in our jobs, hoping to get ahead without getting fired or rejected. Then in our fantasies or times of life planning, we try to ignore the pressure and dream of the day when we can be freer from the whims and demands of bosses and other people.

Life's Uniqueness

Almost twenty years have passed since that day when my wife and I started married life and began our journey across the country. In preparing to write this chapter, I was amazed at the extent to which our lives have fit the patterns that Erikson, Levinson, and others have described.

It is important to remember, however, that no two people are identical. Our journeys through life may have some common turning points, but each of us is unique. We soon discover that events such as a serious illness, the deaths of family members, financial crises, economic depression, wars and conscription into military service, business failure, or unusual vocational success can each retard our progress through life, or accelerate it.

When I was partway through college, I decided to quit school for a year and move to Europe. In looking back, I don't see this as an escape from pressure or boredom—although I did appreciate the change. Instead, my time overseas was a liberating chance to pull away for a while and to think about my life and future. In contrast, there are people who drop out for so long a period that they never come back to the mainstream of life. Still others become what once were called "organization men"—people who give themselves completely to a career (perhaps even to a church-related career), even if this means a sacrifice of marital stability, family life, or creative thinking.

Young adulthood can be a mixture of crisis, turmoil, challenge, and growth. How you move through this period depends on how you handle change. That is what table 1-1 is all about. Much depends on how you deal with the issues we have discussed in this chapter and others that will be considered in the following pages. Wherever he or she is in life, each adult can benefit from periodic self-appraisal and a look at those skills we need to help us mature. It is to the issues of skills and competence that we turn in the next chapter.

Table 1-1
How to Handle Change

Change is always with us, whether we like it or not. The following are some ideas to keep in mind when you encounter change.

1. Be willing to face the fact that change is sometimes needed; we have to "do something" about a difficult situation.

2. Try to clarify the problem or issue that needs to be changed. Perhaps you can write on paper exactly what the problem is. For example, "I no longer can live in this house," or, "I've got to find a higher-paying job."

3. Ask yourself if there is another way to look at the issue. A friend can often bring a perspective that you do not see.

4. Clearly state your goal. What do you want to happen in the future? Try to be both realistic and specific. For example, "I want to live in a place where my parents will not be free to intervene in my life-style," or, "I want work that is more fulfilling and less boring."

5. Make a list of possible solutions. Put this on paper. Which of your solutions is realistic? Which is practical?

6. Decide on a course of action. Which of the solutions will you attempt first? Specifically, what will you do? When will you act?

7. When you have decided on a course of action, take it!

8. Evaluate what you have done. Have your actions worked to solve a problem or to help you change? If not, go back and look over the above steps. Look especially at step 5. What is another possible solution?

In summary, it is helpful to follow this little chart, starting at the top.

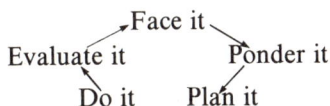

```
                      Face it
                    ↗        ↘
        Evaluate it            Ponder it
                  ↖          
            Do it      Plan it
```

Source Notes

1. D. S. Preston, "Who am I?" *Christianity Today,* vol. 25, November 6, 1981, p. 54, used with permission.

2. This is the title of a book by Roger L. Gould, *Transformations: Growth and Change in Adult Life* (New York: Simon and Schuster, 1978).

3. E. H. Erikson, *Childhood and Society,* 2nd ed. (New York: W. W. Norton, 1963). (The first edition appeared in 1950.)

4. See, for example, E. H. Erikson, *Identity—Youth and Crisis* (New York: W. W. Norton, 1968).

5. D. S. Preston, op. cit.

6. Daniel J. Levinson et al., *The Seasons of a Man's Life* (New York: Alfred A. Knopf, 1978).

7. Ibid., p. 73.

8. Ibid., pp. 57–58, 82, 83.

9. Ibid., p. 86.

10. L. C. Lehman, *Age and Achievement* (Princeton, N.J.: Princeton University Press, 1953).

2

Becoming Competent

Handling Your Struggles and Skills

When I was eighteen, I joined the navy. It wasn't the regular navy; I was only in the reserves while I went to college, but the experience was liberating. After a few weekly training sessions near home, my colleagues and I were sent to the East Coast where we took navigation and seamanship classes, learned about "duty" and military discipline, endured what seemed like endless stupid rules and training activities, and even spent several weeks riding around the Atlantic on what was officially called a cruise. It might have been a cruise, but it was no Love Boat. We worked hard, and for the first time in life most of us discovered what it was like to live away from home.

The desire for independence probably was one of my reasons for joining the navy. Although I appreciated my family, I was ready for the freedom that we expected to find in the service. But I wasn't ready for the discovery that complete independence is a myth. We human beings are affected by one another whether we like it or not.

Regardless of our age or stage in life, each of us is influenced by others in at least three ways. First, there are the personal influences that come from family, fellow students, friends, the people at work or in our church, neighbors, and those who serve us in stores or restaurants. In the navy, many miles from home, my parents weren't around to influence me directly (even though I was aware of the values they had taught), but I was influenced by the officers I met and by the other recruits with whom I lived and worked.

I was also influenced by "the system"—those government rules and regulations that determined how I dressed, where I lived, and how I spent my time. Civilians, of course, are free of military regulations, but there are other institutional influences that affect us—at least indirectly. The mass media, the Internal Revenue Service, the laws of the land, the votes of government leaders, the state of the economy, the presence or absence of crime in our neighborhoods—each has an important bearing on how we live. If the government raises taxes, the college cuts off scholarships, the garbage collectors go on strike, or the city tears up the street to put in a new sewer, we will be affected, probably inconvenienced, and maybe annoyed.

Although we may not think much about this, we are also controlled by cultural influences. One dictionary defines culture as the sum total of those ways of living that have been built up by a group of human beings and that are passed from one generation to the next. The military culture, for example, involves such things as the wearing of uniforms, the separation of people into ranks, saluting, and the use of technical and slang terms that civilians don't understand. For all of us, culture guides our thinking, lets us know what is considered right and wrong, teaches us how to dress and behave in social situations, influences how and whether we will celebrate holidays such as Christmas, and teaches us about values such as honesty, fairness, or how to handle competition. Cultural rules rarely are written in any book, and it is unlikely that we would be arrested for ignoring cultural standards. Nevertheless, these social rules are taught in our homes and schools, and followed faithfully by most people in the society. When we travel to another country and experience culture shock, we are encountering the fact that not everybody "does things" the way we do. Even at home, cultural expectations are always changing, especially in this age when the media introduce us so dramatically and so effectively to other societies. In spite of the changes, however, most of us find that life is a little easier to understand and handle because we understand our own cultures.[1]

These three groups of influences—personal, institutional, and cultural—overlap. They affect each other, and they affect us all as we move into and through adulthood.

If adults are to succeed in their careers, communicate effectively, reach life goals, solve problems, manage their daily lives, and get along with people, there are two things that *must* be learned. First, we must learn to know and to understand the people, institutions, and culture that influence us. Second, we must learn competence in a variety of skills, including self-management skills, communication skills, problem-solving skills, and goal-setting skills.[2] One of the main purposes of this book is to consider the knowledge and skills that are needed by young adults.

To begin, it might be helpful to consider some of the attitudes and thoughts that many people have as they move through the twenties. We have determined already that each person is unique, but there are similarities that everybody experiences, both because of human physiology and because of society's three groups of influences.

Looking Within

Unlike any previous generation, young adults today have grown up in what Martin Gross has called the "psychological society."[3] It could be argued, perhaps, that interest in psychology is waning, but psychology courses still are popular on college campuses, and psychological books—including waves of self-help books—continue to flood the market, along with a variety of seminars, awareness exercises, stress-management programs, and innovations in psychotherapy. All of this has made us aware of feelings and frustrations. Such awareness can be harmful, if we let ourselves slide into morbid introspection, but self-awareness can also be a healthy step toward personal maturity and emotional stability.

When we reach young adulthood, most of us are aware of our increased freedom. At last, we have grown up and are accepted by a society that is willing to treat us as adults. We are less controlled by parents and freer to make decisions. All of this is liberating. But we are also freer to fail. Now we must handle our own finances and there may be a nervous discomfort about career choices. Soon we learn that life is neither simple nor fair. Circumstances cannot always be controlled, and people sometimes cannot be trusted. Education and hard work do not always bring career success, and bodies—even young bodies—sometimes break down and get sick.

Older people might be discouraged by such thoughts, but that is not true of most young adults. According to one writer,[4] young adults tend to have an inner optimism; a belief that problems will be overcome and that goals can be reached. Although depression and disillusionment tend to be common in this period, there still is a resiliency and sense of self-confidence that lets young adults "retain a basic sense of trust in themselves and their own potential. Even after the most painful confrontations and greatest disappointments they are typically able to pick themselves up, pull themselves together and prepare to try again."[5]

For many people at this age, there is a new realization of the community's importance and sometimes this leads to an active involvement in causes that could make things better. Unlike the adolescent, who tends to dwell on his or her own personal worries and concerns, the young adult can look at life more objectively and can see value in "seeing ourselves as others see us." Often there is idealism (which doesn't modify until later in life) along with an openness to new ideas and a willingness to try unconventional or untested approaches to solving problems. "Young adults bring to familiar situations an enthusiasm, an energy, and a confidence that enhance and strengthen their freshness of approach," one observer has written. "In contrast to older adults, young adults have not already encountered the frustrations and disappointments of unsuccessfully trying to solve complex problems of daily life. They see not an old, chronic problem but one for which new ideas and new developments may bring new avenues of hope and new modes of attack."[6]

Sometimes it is more difficult to bring these fresh perspectives on to our own problems. Throughout life, for example, most of us struggle with our self-image, and this issue is especially acute as we begin our adult years. The self-image—what we think about ourselves—is usually kept hidden. Nobody can know what you think about yourself unless you choose to tell somebody, or unless your actions give clues about what you think. Most of us realize this, so we try to hide our insecurities, sexual preferences, doubts, feelings, and attitudes behind a mask that says all is well and everything in life is under control. In our hearts we know that everybody has struggles and feelings of incompetence, but we are reluctant to admit this—even to ourselves—at a time when there is a lot of competition to succeed as an adult.

Sometimes it can be interesting to take a piece of paper, write the words *I am. . .* , and then complete the sentence with as many adjectives as you can think of to describe yourself.

This list will give a good indication of your self-image. If you are like most people, there will be positive and negative words on the list, and if you decide to show the list to someone who knows you well, the other person's reaction to your list might be surprising. This picture we have of ourselves is important, because it strongly influences both how we act, especially when we are with others, and how we handle ourselves as adults. It is encouraging to recognize that the self-image can change. Each of life's experiences can modify the self-image and so can our contacts with other people, our introspections, and our periods of prayer and meditation on spiritual issues. The self-image and ability to get along well in society also changes when we develop the competencies that come with the learning of new skills.

Learning Life Skills

When I was in high school, I was required to take courses in French, but I never studied any Spanish. This has presented some difficulties, especially when I am in Hispanic communities, so I recently decided to enroll in a Spanish course. To put it mildly, my progress has been slow, but I've stuck with the program because I am motivated to learn at least the basics of what for me is a new language.

Learning a new language involves the acquisition of a skill. Until we learn how to communicate verbally, as well as non-verbally, it is difficult to get along with people. Most of childhood is spent learning the skills that we need to survive and succeed in the world where we live. As we get older, we learn how to date (that is a learned skill), how to study for exams, how to make decisions or solve problems, how to manage time and money, how to think clearly, how to deal with anger, how to cope with stress, and how we can grow spiritually. Some of these skills are learned from books, many result from personal experience, and others come through the teaching and encouragement of other people. Much of education involves learning skills, and many of life's failures come because we have not learned the skills needed to get along in this complex society. It probably is true that most people want to *be competent* and to *feel competent* in the tasks of getting along with others,[7] but such competence only comes when we continue to learn the skills of living as we move into adulthood.

In seminars on young adulthood, I sometimes ask people to list the major problems of this time in life. The responses are almost always thought-provoking.

How can I build a good relationship with my dad?

How do I decide values for myself without automatically accepting my parents' values?

How can I be patient?

With the college years passing so quickly, how do I slow my life down?

How do I cope with old friends from high school? I don't want to hurt them, but I am changed.

I struggle with my career. Have I made the right choice? Can I still change if I want to?

How do I find a mate?

I can't understand my roommate! What do I do?

How can I manage my time?

Is it possible to compete for job promotions and still serve God?

To solve the problems these questions raise, we must become increasingly competent in at least six different skill areas.[8] But don't let this scare you. Before we leave high school, we've already made a lot of progress in sharpening these skills, and in time most people learn to handle the complexities of adulthood. We deal with this period of life more effectively, however, when we are knowledgeable about the challenges ahead and when we make some effort to learn the skills that we need to be successful.

Physical Skills. By the time we reach adulthood, we should know how to take care of our bodies. We have learned about exercise, eating a balanced diet, effective grooming, and the need to get sufficient sleep. What we know, however, isn't always translated into action. People who know about the harmful effects of drugs and alcohol nevertheless indulge, sometimes excessively. We who hear so much about weight often eat too much and get out of shape before we are thirty. Each October, at the school where I teach, a number of students sign up for recreational football programs. These people have the best of intentions, but because they are not in good physical condition, several end up on crutches or with arms in slings.

When we are young, most of us act as if our bodies will last forever. We know that isn't true, of course, but young bodies can take a lot of punishment and they have a way of rejuvenating quickly. For many it is a mark of success and a way to find acceptance if we let people know that our bodies can perform athletic feats, handle large quantities of alcohol, or fit into bikinis. Sometimes, without thinking much about the physical consequences, we push ourselves to the limit, embrace unhealthy crash diets, or use beauty aids that do more harm than good.

As a psychologist, I am neither qualified nor inclined to tell you how to take care of yourself physically. I can remind you, however, that tired, overweight, and sluggish bodies do not function at top efficiency. It is difficult to study effectively, develop relationships with others, manage stress, and build a career if we ignore the bodies that house our brain power. If you are a Christian, you may remember Paul's straightforward comments in his first letter to the Corinthians. Our bodies, he said, belong to God. The Holy Spirit lives within us, and we have a responsibility both to take care of ourselves and to honor God with our bodies (1 Corinthians 6:13–15, 19, 20).

One physical skill that we often do not encounter during adolescence is the need to relax our bodies. Everybody knows that we live in a time of great stress and often the pressures of living make our muscles literally "uptight." The two tables that accompany this chapter deal with physical and emotional tension. They are designed to help you relax physically and mentally.

Intellectual/Problem-Solving Skills.   In their interviews with reporters, professional athletes often talk about the need to be mentally alert if one is to succeed in sports. Even when their bodies are in top shape and their athletic skills are developed to a high level of competence, these professionals know the importance of concentration and mental attitude.

To develop mental competence is one of the major purposes of schools. It distresses us to discover that "Johnny can't read" and that college students can't write. We know that the ability to learn efficiently, to communicate effectively, and to think clearly are all crucial if we are to handle stress and adapt to change.

After we leave high school, to a large extent our vocations determine which intellectual skills we need to develop. Chemists and other research scientists must learn to think scientifically. The physician, the mechanic, the maintenance man, and the person who repairs TV sets must each learn how to diagnose problems and determine the best treatment. The counselor must learn to be sensitive to people. The artist or interior decorator must be alert to color. The teacher and preacher must know something about communication skills and ways to convey information and new learning. It probably is true that successful people are always learning and looking for ways to improve their vocational skills.

One intellectual skill that is needed by people in all vocations is the ability to solve problems. At the risk of oversimplification it might be suggested that problem solving involves a few basic steps. First, there is *clarification*. This is the need to get a clear picture of what the problem really is. It is good to be as specific as possible. "I can't get along with my roommate" is vague. "My roommate and I disagree over our tastes in music" is more specific and gives you something to work on.

Next, try some *goal setting*. Specifically, what would you like to see happen? Maybe you would "like to work out a compromise so we could each listen to the music we like, without pushing our preferences onto each other and without arguing." Just as it is not always easy to clarify the problem, so it sometimes is difficult to determine what would be a workable solution that really could make things better. Sometimes it helps to discuss this with a friend who can clarify your thinking.

Then you can do some *exploration of possible solutions*. Some people find it helpful to write these down. Decide what might work and then ponder what you might do to implement your plan. Ask yourself if your plan is realistic, feasible, specific. Then *implement the proposed solution*. With that roommate you may decide to move out, propose that you only play music when one of you is away, or suggest that you each get a set of earphones to plug into your personal stereos.

The final stage is *evaluation*. Did your plan work? If not, try to determine both what went wrong and how you could try again in the future and be more successful.

The solving of problems can be complicated and often more difficult than we have implied. In finding solutions there frequently is a need for creativity, persistence, and the insights of others. At times we must recognize that some problems cannot be solved, but must be accepted. Learning to live with a difficult situation also involves skills, including self-management skills.

Self-management Skills. After I had been teaching for several years, I decided that the time had come for a change. I enjoyed the interaction with students, my colleagues were friendly, and the school was a pleasant place to work. But I was tired of committees, faculty meetings, long appointments to discuss student theses, and the endless reading of papers. After a lot of careful deliberation, I had lunch with the dean, resigned my tenure, shifted to a part-time position, and moved out to work independently as a psychologist and writer.

I had expected that it would take a while to get used to my new freedom, so I wasn't upset when a week or two went by and I hadn't done any work. When a month went by, however, followed by another, and then a third, I almost panicked. I found myself swamped by interruptions. The telephone was one culprit, and so were the interruptions from former students. I had to recognize, however, that the chief villain was me. I was interrupting myself, daydreaming, making phone calls, and getting distracted by projects that didn't need to be done immediately. My reduced paycheck jolted me into the realization that I had better get control of my time or the whole family would starve.

My problem was one of self-discipline. I had to learn to

manage myself and my time. I used all kinds of gimmicks to keep myself at work. I cut out luncheon meetings, for example, only took telephone calls between nine and ten in the morning, counted the time I actually spent at my desk (but deducted the time spent in daydreaming, making coffee in the kitchen, looking at the comics, or wandering down the hall to the bathroom), and didn't go to bed until I had put in at least eight hours. Some of these techniques seemed silly—especially when I would reward myself for some accomplishment—but my reading in time-management books convinced me that most people have similar problems when there is no boss around, and most of us have to use gimmicks if we are to keep time from slipping away.

Self-discipline and the control of time are only two of the self-management skills that we need to learn in adulthood. In this age of easy credit we must learn to control our use of credit cards. We must learn to manage money and to plan our careers. The regular exercise and balanced diet that we mentioned earlier only become part of our lives when we learn some self-control. Some people don't learn very well. In contrast, others are so controlled that they are rigid. Much better is the ability to manage our lives and our time efficiently but with freedom to be spontaneous. Otherwise, life is so structured that it isn't any fun.

Interpersonal Skills.   Getting along with people is one of the most difficult challenges of life. It doesn't take long even for the young child to discover that people differ from one another in their desires, values, beliefs, interests, habits, personality characteristics, opinions, life-styles, goals, and ways of doing things. These differences cannot be ignored, and it is not often that we can fight them. Instead, we have to adapt to one another and learn to get along. That takes determination, skill, hard work, and sometimes a lot of patience. The biblical writer was realistic when he instructed his readers: "If it is possible, as far as it depends on you, live at peace with everyone" (Romans 12:18).

Many of the tasks of young adulthood involve interpersonal skills. Getting launched in a career, finding a mate, building a marriage, starting a family, getting along in the community, becoming involved in a church—all involve such "people skills" as learning to listen, being able to communicate clearly, knowing how to resist manipulation, and acting appropriately in social situations. Each of these skills involves knowledge (knowing how to respond) and action (doing what is appropriate). Each takes time and effort to learn.

Emotional Skills. Everybody knows that it takes a lot of practice to play tennis well, to type efficiently, or to perform a piano concerto. These are learned skills that take time and effort to acquire.

Emotions, in contrast, are a part of human nature and sometimes appear when they are least expected. It doesn't take much skill to feel sad or to experience disappointment, anger, excitement, or the pain of frustration. In themselves, such feelings have little to do with learning.

What we do learn is how to recognize feelings, how to control them, and how to express them appropriately. We must learn to be sensitive to our own feelings and to the feelings of others. We must learn where to express our feelings and how to express them within the cultural expectations of our society. Where and when, for example is it socially acceptable to cry, to laugh aloud, or to shout, "Hurray"? None of this may seem very important, but if we are unaware of our feelings, and unable to express them, we often experience serious emotional and social difficulties.

Spiritual Skills. Within recent years the Western world has seen an upsurge of interest in Eastern forms of meditation, altered states of consciousness, and self-awareness programs. Most of this interest has been among young adults, many of whom are looking for greater meaning and purpose in life. Classes in yoga, transcendental meditation, and self-hypnosis seek to help people both relax and attain awareness of powers or beings greater than themselves. Such classes are teaching both knowledge and the skills of relating to spiritual forces that are assumed to exist.

Christians assume that we relate to a Person—Jesus Christ. We tend to resist the idea of "spiritual skills," but even the disciples asked Jesus how to pray, and the Scriptures are filled with examples and instructions of ways by which we grow in a relationship with God. Everyone can pray; no training program is needed. Anyone can read the Bible or attend church. Soon we recognize, however, that the past and present spiritual giants all developed skills in managing time so they could communicate with God. All learned how to pray more effectively, how to study Scripture, how to meditate on devotional literature, how to worship, and how to stimulate spiritual growth in themselves and others. These are spiritual skills that the Christian spends a lifetime learning—and never completes the job.

Laying the Foundation

Young adulthood has been described as a period of time when we lay the foundation for the remainder of life.[9] Like the carpenter or bricklayer who uses skills to build a house, so the life builder relies on skills to build relationships, to get established, and to make his mark on the world.

This life building in young adulthood involves several tasks, many of which take place simultaneously. Except for those who marry at a very young age there is the challenge of learning to live as a single adult. Other tasks may include selecting a mate and building a marriage; deciding whether or not to have children and in many cases starting a family; adjusting, when necessary, to widowhood or divorced status; selecting a vocation and building a career; becoming more involved in society; settling into an adult life-style; dealing with failures and frustrations; and moving into the middle-age years. Each of the remaining chapters of this book deals with one of these tasks. In each chapter there is an emphasis on what you need to know and the skills you might want to develop. At times we will draw on the conclusions of Erikson or Levinson, but we will also consider the work of other writers and the emphasis will be on the practical.

Not all of the chapters will speak to you at the present stage in your journey through life. If you are in the process of building a marriage, the chapter on being a single adult probably won't interest you (except perhaps when you get really frustrated with your mate), but it might help you to understand friends who are facing a marriage breakup. If you are nineteen, the chapter on middle age may not seem very relevant, although it can be helpful to think ahead. If you choose to skip over some of the chapters, please look at the tables as you pass by. These are designed to give brief overviews of practical issues that could concern all of us, regardless of our stage in life.

It would be wrong to assume that most people leave high school and launch immediately into learning new skills and building the foundation for an adult life. For a lot of us, our twenties are a time to drop out for a while and take a breather between the hectic teens and the established living of middle age.

Some people drop out by escaping.[10] They struggle with authority, grapple with morality, and sometimes adopt unconventional life-styles. Others become rigid, refuse to try anything new, and as a result become stagnant. These people get into a rut and stop growing. A third group decides to suspend normal activities for a year or so but has every intention of returning to the mainstream later. These are the people who drop out of college to do manual labor or who take a few months to wander around Europe before starting graduate school. Some of this drop-out time can be healthy, providing the breather period doesn't last too long.

It is difficult for me to write about this with objectivity. I'm biased, because at the age of twenty-three, I chose to take the breather that was mentioned earlier. I was tired of school, so I worked all summer, bought a one-way ticket to Europe (I couldn't afford a round-trip ticket), and took off. The time away gave me the opportunity to live in other countries, to experience the rich cultural heritage of Europe, and to think through my own values and future direction. This isn't good for everyone, but it gave me a new lease on life and a fresh impetus to return to the tasks of laying the foundation of my adult life.

A Concluding Comment

A well-known biblical parable is the story of the talents, recorded in Matthew 25. Three people were given money to take care of during their employer's absence. Two of the employees invested the money wisely; the third was criticized because he hid what he had and accomplished nothing.

The practical application is obvious. In His infinite wisdom, God has given each person a supply of talents, gifts, abilities, and opportunities. At the end of life, some will have used their talents well; others will have lived wasted lives.

What we do with our God-given gifts depends somewhat on how we handle the pull between risk and security. Paul Tournier, the famous Swiss counselor, has written about the trapeze performer who has to let go of one swing before he or she can move on to the next. The letting go involves risk. Hanging on gives security but there is no progress. As Christians, our challenge is to take careful risks, avoiding reckless abandon, but refusing to dry up in the security of inactivity. In every decision of life, we are faced with the choice of staying where we are or risking something new and different. The more we take risks, the more opportunity there is for growth—and for failure.

At the basis of every adult decision and every risk, there is the important question of values: what we believe, what we consider to be right and wrong, and what we think is really important in life. We cannot push these issues to the back of our minds because they influence almost everything we do and color every decision. We will discuss them further in the next chapter.

Table 2-1
How to Cope With Stress

Have you ever wondered why some people reach middle life and find themselves overweight, out of shape, and perpetually tense? When they were twenty years younger, some of these same people may have criticized the pressure-filled, middle-age life-style with its concern about mortgages, money, marital tensions, career pressures, and the hassles of raising teenagers. These problems tend to creep up on us, and we have difficulty coping if we never learned how to handle stress when we were younger. The many books on stress management list some basic principles that can be learned early in life. These principles include the following.[11]

1. Take care of yourself physically. Regular exercise, a balanced diet, and sufficient rest help to rejuvenate us and enable us to think more clearly in times of stress. Don't forget to take time off periodically. The old biblical injunction of taking off one day each week is good advice.

2. Stay away from the harmful "solutions." It is not true that alcohol or other drugs will solve your stress problems. These help us escape for a while but they do nothing to deal with the causes of stress, and often drugs create stresses of their own. Yoga, transcendental meditation, and Eastern religions will calm the body, but their practice is surely inconsistent with biblical teaching and not recommended for Christians.

3. Ponder the causes of your stress. Can you do anything to change your circumstances and eliminate some of the stresses? Think about your priorities. Do you take on too many assignments and then wonder why you run out of time? What can you change in your life in order to reduce stress?

4. Consider your attitudes. Are you a perfectionist, unable to laugh at life, unwilling to make changes, too insecure to

confront problems? Have you convinced yourself that you are incompetent, stupid, or unable to handle the stress? Is there any evidence for such conclusions? How can you change these attitudes? Can another person help you?

5. Use your spiritual resources. Don't overlook the importance of prayer and meditation on the Scriptures. Ask God to give you patience, strength, and wisdom.

6. Get some help. Often other people can bring a fresh perspective and creative solutions to our problems. A friend, a clergyman, a professional counselor—each can be helpful. Sometimes these helpers give us assistance now and teach us how to handle stress in the future.

Table 2-2
How to Relax

Every introductory psychology book describes the "fight or flight syndrome." When an animal is confronted with danger there are physiological changes within the body. The muscles get tense, the heart beats faster, adrenaline surges into the bloodstream. All of this prepares the animal for a fight or for flight away from the danger.

When humans feel threatened, our bodies also are aroused, but it isn't always appropriate for us to fight or to run away. Because of this, our bodies remain in a state of tension. If the tension persists, we develop ulcers, blood pressure goes up, or the body shows signs of breaking down in other ways.

The ultimate solution for all of this is to find and eliminate the causes of the stress. At times, however, we are so keyed up physically that we can't think clearly enough to do our work or to tackle the pressures. It helps both physically and mentally if we can learn to relax, by using some of the following techniques.[12]

1. Determine to relax. This isn't as obvious a starting place as it may seem. Some people seem to enjoy tension, even though their bodies do not. When they relax, these people feel guilty. Recognize that it is both healthy and wise to relax. But don't try so hard to relax that you create more tension.

2. Find a place to relax. It helps if you can find a quiet environment where you will be free of interruptions for a while. Loosen tight clothing and try to get into a relaxed position. Try to develop a "passive attitude." This involves letting yourself unwind without worrying about time or about how well you are relaxing.

3. Loosen your muscles. Tighten the muscles in your toes two or three times and then relax them. Repeat this as you move slowly up the body. Pause periodically to breathe

deeply. Taking deep breaths can be helpful in itself and this is something you can do to relax yourself during the day.

4. Use your imagination. For a while, imagine that you are in some relaxed environment, away from the pressures of life.

5. Take time for some diversions. What you do will depend on you. For some people watching a television comedy is relaxing; others like to play golf, or strum a guitar. Be careful not to let these diversionary activities create tension. If you get uptight over golf scores, this is not relaxing.

6. Meditate. Avoid transcendental meditation because of its non-Christian base. Don't aim to empty your mind of all thought. Instead take the time to meditate on the Bible. Read Psalms 1:1, 2 then give some thought to Philippians 4:6–8. Ask God to show you Scripture verses that are especially helpful.

Source Notes

1. Sociology and psychology students will recognize that this section of the book is discussing systems theory—the idea that each of us is part of and influenced by a series of social systems. For a discussion of systems theory as it applies to young adulthood, see Gerard Egan and Michael Cowan, *People in Systems: A Model for Development in the Human-Service Professions and Education* (Monterey, Calif.: Brooks/Cole, 1979); and Gerard Egan and Michael A. Cowan, *Moving Into Adulthood* (Monterey, Calif.: Brooks/Cole, 1980).

2. The development of life skills, including the development of these four skills, is a major theme of the two Egan and Cowan books.

3. See Martin L. Gross, *The Psychological Society* (New York: Simon and Schuster, 1978).

4. Gene Bocknek, *The Young Adult: Development After Adolescence* (Monterey, Calif.: Brooks/Cole, 1980).

5. Ibid., p. 111.

6. Ibid., p. 117.

7. Egan and Cowan, *People in Systems,* p. 42.

8. The following paragraphs are adapted from the 1979 Egan and Cowan book, pp. 44–58.

9. Naomi Golan, *Passing Through Transitions: A Guide for Practitioners* (New York: The Free Press, 1981).

10. W. Perry, *Forms of Intellectual and Ethical Development in the College Years* (New York: Holt, Rinehart & Winston, 1970).

11. Adapted from two books by Gary R. Collins, *Relax and Live Longer* and *Spotlight on Stress.* Both are published by Vision House, Ventura, California, the former in 1977, the latter in 1982.

12. For further information, please see the two books by Collins listed above; Herbert Benson's *The Relaxation Response* (New York: William Morrow, 1975); John D. Curtis and Richard A. Detert, *How to Relax* (Palo Alto, Calif.: Mayfield Publishing Company, 1981); or Martha Davis, Matthew McKay, and Elizabeth Robbins Eshelman, *The Relaxation and Stress Reduction Workbook* (Richmond, Calif.: New Harbinger Publications, 1980).

3

Becoming Independent

Handling Your Identity and Need for Intimacy

Are you a part of the baby-boom or post-baby-boom generation?

If you were born after 1945 and are old enough to read this book, the answer to that question is probably yes.

Following World War II, the birth rate rose dramatically. Military service had ended, a marriage boom had begun, and thousands of couples were making up for lost time by starting their families. Pregnancy, it seemed, was patriotic, and to the surprise of no one, the infant population swelled to record highs.

The real surprise came a few years later when the sociologists and demographers noticed that the postwar population explosion wasn't slowing down. In the 1950s, most nations had returned to their prewar birth rates, but four countries—Canada, Australia, New Zealand, and the United States—saw the baby boom continue. It wasn't until the mid-sixties that birth rates slowed down in these countries and that "zero population growth" became a popular rallying cry. Those who most loudly proclaimed "ZPG" were the first baby boomers who, by that time, had reached college age and were busy turning campuses into battlegrounds of turmoil and protest.

All of this might be boring and of limited interest, except for the fact that the postwar population boom has affected every aspect of society, including education, music, entertainment, fads, fashions, and our views about such issues as religion, marriage, divorce, sex, child rearing, work, politics, abortion, and standards of right and wrong. The baby boomers—those born between the mid-forties and the mid-sixties—have been called "the biggest, richest, and best educated generation America has ever produced...," blessed with "great expectations of affluence and education," and "raised as a generation of idealism and hope." It also appears to be a generation of uncertainty, fierce competitiveness, and intense frustration.[1]

As they reach adulthood, baby boomers are discovering that education does not produce endless job opportunities or an abundance of money and professional recognition. There is limited room at the top and a lot of people competing to get there. Many who were raised in an era of affluence, optimism, and the unrealistic values of television, now find themselves struggling to get jobs, to get ahead, to buy houses, and to adjust to a lower-than-expected standard of living. As frustrations persist, and as long-established moral standards are questioned, the crime rate has risen, and so has the prevalence of divorce, family violence, depression, and suicide.

This is the first generation to live with future shock—something that Alvin Toffler defines as "the human response to overstimulation"[2]—a reaction to too much change coming too quickly. As a nation, we have thrown off the rigid and stifling attitudes of our Victorian ancestors, but we have been left with an era of uncertainty, a lack of commitment to much of anything, and widespread stress.

All of us who live in the midst of the boom generation are affected by its influence. That includes those of us who arrived before 1945 and those younger people who have grown up in the shadow of that massive, tumultuous, constantly changing, and slightly older generation that is ahead. It is into this world that young adults are trying to fit.

According to the Bible, Adam lived by himself for a while, but he was lonely and wanted a companion. From that time to the present, almost nobody has lived in complete isolation. The presence of a baby-boom generation affects us all, but that is not the only influence on young adults today. All of our lives are molded by economic conditions, political circumstances, the availability or nonavailability of jobs or food, the adequacy of local medical care and police protection, the quality of the environment where we live, the state of our health, and the actions and attitudes of our parents and friends. In moving from adolescence into adulthood each person must be alert to cultural and community influences, but within that setting, each of us must also resolve several practical issues if we want to become independent and mature adults.

Becoming Self-Sufficient

One of the major tasks of young adulthood is to build a different kind of relationship with parents. For much of our lives, our parents have taken care of us, given us a place to live, freely commented on our values, provided for us financially, and had an influence on our time and activities. During the teenage years, there may have been some disagreements if you tried to exert your independence, but you were still "a kid" and not often able to get adult treatment. Now that you are "a grown-up," you and your parents must learn to get along as equals. Instead of being financially and emotionally dependent on your parents, you must become more self-sufficient. Ideally, everyone should work to build a mutual interdependence between the adult members of the family.

For many families, such a change is not easy. Consider, for example, how some people have described their struggles:

> I've got a major problem right now with my parents. I'm the oldest and am trying to make my own decisions, but when I feel I make a good decision, they don't necessarily agree. It's hard to keep communication lines open and honest, and this is very frustrating.

> I'm twenty-one and have put myself through two years of college, but it seems my parents still want to run my life. At what point can we say "this is my life—you can't tell me what to do"?

> How can I break away from my parents and get some freedom? I don't want to hurt anyone.

> I've just returned from college after not being an active part of my family for the last three years. Now I am living at home again while I prepare to go to grad school. I'm truly struggling with knowing how much time to invest in my family versus investing time in current friendships. I anticipate being married one day and I'm not exactly sure how to integrate my priorities of career, future marriage, personal interests, and the family I grew up in.

> Being part of a close-knit, loving, Godly family and having all the things that come along with young adulthood like school and a serious dating relationship, how do I show my family that I love them even though other things are becoming seemingly more important?

> How do you get over leaving home when you love it so much? Why do I feel like I am making my folks sad or "old" because I am leaving them?

I've got just one parent, my mother, and since I'm the only
son, how do I view the relationship and what are my obliga-
tions? I'm twenty.

My parents keep telling me what it was like when they were
young. Then they expect me to be perfect.

It is not surprising that young adults and their parents often
have different and sometimes conflicting values, attitudes, and
perspectives on life. In past generations, parents had a greater
part in molding their children, but within recent years, the
media (especially television), the increased ease and broad-
ening effect of travel, and the upsurge in educational opportunities have all encouraged young people to think more
independently. Often this thinking is at variance with parental
values and that creates conflict, especially when the young
adult chooses to live at home.

It may be helpful to recognize that the move to self-sufficiency often hurts. Like surgery that causes discomfort before
it brings healing, the cutting of parental ties often is accompanied by pain, tension, and loneliness. All separations—including the separation from a family—bring a sense of loss, a
grieving for what must be given up. There is fear that the future may not be as good as the past, accompanied by a realization that the future could be even better.[3] The move to
self-sufficiency involves risk, and risk is never easy.

Nevertheless, there are some steps you can take to ease the
transition. First, try to see things from your parents' perspective. Your move to greater independence may be harder for
them than it is for you. If they are like most parents, they want
the best for you. But sometimes parents also want their own
independence. They have spent twenty or more years raising
children, and although they may not mention or even recognize this, some may feel a resentment that adult children are

still living at home, making demands, and preventing parents from enjoying additional freedom. Most parents, I suspect, have an urge to protect their children, as they have done in the past, and some may try to control and influence their adult off-spring, not necessarily because you need it, but because your parents have a need to feel useful. At times they may attempt to control you by making you feel guilty—and many don't even realize that this is what they are doing.

As you move into adulthood, there can be value in giving serious consideration to the opinions and perspectives of your parents. Surely their experience is of some value. Ultimately, however, you must make your own decisions and be willing to live with the consequences. If you continue to respect their point of view, while you stick with your own, then your times of disagreement may be a little less tense, frequent, or combative.

It may help, too, if you decide what you can overlook. I remember visiting a home where the mother treated her teenage sons as if they were little kids. "Don't forget to get a clean handkerchief, Johnny," she called as one of the boys was leaving. "Take a jacket in case it gets cold."

I am well aware that the boys may have said nothing because there was a visitor in the house, but I had the impression that they simply tolerated their mother's mannerisms, reserving arguments for things that were more important. Some things just have to be overlooked. You won't be home forever.

Recognize, however, that parents need to give and to understand too. Try to help them see your point of view without demanding that they agree. As you are well aware, some parents are more willing to work at understanding and communication than are others. When parents are excessively critical and inclined to intrude in your life without paying much attention to your opinion, or when parents seem to lose all interest in you as soon as you leave home, then a good mutual relationship is difficult to build. It is probable, however, that most parents are in between these two extremes, and are willing to listen if you are not too pushy, impatient, or resentful of their ideas. There will be times, certainly, when you and your parents decide that no agreement is possible, but even talking about this is a step in the right direction of maturity.

If you choose to live at home, you can expect that the route to self-sufficiency will be harder. The people who own the house and pay the bills have a right to set the rules. You may not agree with this, but you are not likely to get very far if you resist. It probably is true that real self-sufficiency cannot come as long as you live at home and remain at least partially dependent on your parents' financial support. Even if you pay all of your bills, you still have to live by the rules of the "management," especially if you have chosen by your own free will to live there.

Whether you live at home or chose to move out, you may find that in your family everybody really wants to make a smooth transition. There may be a willingness to cooperate, a sincere desire to encourage and respect one another, and good communication. This is not some fantasy ideal. It is a realistic possibility that comes when nobody feels threatened and when everybody works at communicating, sharing frustrations in a spirit of love and care, and trying to get along.

Paul's advice may be helpful at this point. "If it is possible," we read in Romans 12:18, 19, "as far as it depends on you, live at peace with everyone. Do not take revenge. . . " Sometimes getting along isn't possible, but make sure that the problem isn't because of your stubbornness, excessive demands, or desire to get even.

Real self-sufficiency does not involve a stubborn demand that you do things your way. The truly self-sufficient person tries to make wise decisions, plans carefully, and works to find a balance between self-direction and sensitivity to the needs of others.[4] The process of separation from parents and movement to self-sufficiency is never really complete.[5] It continues throughout adulthood, but when you understand it and work at it, the process is much smoother than it would be otherwise.

I once knew a young man whose father was a physician and whose family wanted the son to follow in the father's footsteps. In his desire to be independent, the son refused to go to medical school although he recognized, secretly, that he really did want to become a doctor. One day it dawned on him that by trying to be self-sufficient, he was hurting himself and undermining his own career. So he changed his mind and went to medical school, not because his parents insisted, but because of his own self-sufficient decision.

Be careful that you don't sabotage yourself and your future while you try to assert your independence. Sometimes, a self-sufficient decision will be at odds with the views of others, but at other times you can think and act like the people around you and still be self-sufficient. Others may think you are being pushed; you know what you have decided and why.

It would be easy to conclude that self-sufficiency is something you either have or do not have, but that isn't usually what happens. We grow in self-sufficiency as we mature, and often we move ahead in some areas more quickly than in others. A college student, for example, might be very independent in making decisions about courses, but dependent in expecting parents to supply money or to do laundry.

Building Identity

Just as the move to greater self-sufficiency is slow and sometimes lifelong, so is the building of an identity. It might be easy to conclude that after the identity crisis of adolescence, nobody thinks much further about who they are or where they are going. Most of us know that this isn't what happens. The question of identity, consciously or unconsciously considered, is a central concern of young adulthood. The development of an identity has been called the key issue around which the entire process of human development revolves.[6] Your identity influences and in turn is influenced by almost every decision you make at this time of life.

Your identity is the mental picture you have of yourself. Largely built out of your lifelong observations of how other people see you and treat you, identity could be thought of as a collection of your goals, interests, attitudes, beliefs, hopes, values, personality traits, aptitudes, and abilities as you see them.

When we are younger and all of this collection is changing, our identities are in a great state of flux. This can be so confusing, that many people find it easiest simply to go along with the values and expectations of their parents or friends. The college student who accepts the beliefs of a cult or more traditional religion without giving these beliefs much thought, may be an example of someone who is accepting an identity that was created by someone else. The same might be true of the son who reluctantly accepts a secure job in the family business simply because everybody expects this, or the married woman who squelches her interest in a career and adopts the role of a full-time housewife. Such people have accepted the values and decisions of others without thinking them through to see if they really "fit." Because there is no deep personal commitment to these decisions, they often are questioned or abandoned in later life—sometimes to the surprise and distress of others.[7]

Although it is common to experience confusion about our identities in early adulthood, most of us discover that we soon begin to get a clearer perspective of issues such as our goals, attitudes, and values. After what may be a long and sometimes vacillating period of exploration we slowly settle on what we believe, recognize what we can do well, and begin to set some priorities. As this happens, our identities become clearer to ourselves and to others.

If we look at identity in this way, it is easier to see why decisions made in the late teens or early twenties often seem unwise a few years later. Teenage marriages frequently have difficulty because of the changes in thinking that come to the husband and wife as they mature. Career choices made in the early stages of adulthood often are abandoned and replaced in the late twenties, as one's real identity becomes clearer.

This could lead to the discouraging conclusion that decisions made in young adulthood are likely to be unstable and immature. That isn't necessarily so. Many young decisions are wise and long lasting, but you should be open to the fact that some future change is likely.

The development of your identity will never be final. It probably was in turmoil during adolescence, it may be changing now, it probably will settle as you move into your thirties, and it could undergo another disruption as you reevaluate your priorities in mid-life. If you think about it, you might also recognize that your identity is well established in some areas (you may have a clear view of your religious beliefs, for example), but still fluctuating in some other area (such as your choice of a career or your political preferences).[8]

In the meantime, is there anything you can do to help formulate a clearer identity? At some time you might try writing a few paragraphs to summarize your identity. What are your goals, beliefs, attitudes, interests, and abilities? Keep the paper handy and revise it after a few days. Then show it to somebody who knows you well. Do they agree with your self-picture? How would you like to change? What can you do to change?

Recognize that you will be forced to work on your identity whenever you make a decision, but it helps if you can think about where you are in life and where you are going. It also can be helpful to give serious thought to your values.

Deciding on Values

When a national magazine decided to do a special report on "the baby boomers," one of the articles included profiles of several young adults who were intent on "living the good life." These people worked long hours, and expressed a willingness to take risks, leave their home bases, try something new, make sacrifices, and work for financial independence. As a group they were described as being "disciplined, organized, more than a little selfish and obsessively concerned with the quality of their lives."[9] This description is a summary of the values held by one group of young adults.

A value has been described as some belief or way of thinking that we prize even in public, choose freely and deliberately from among several alternatives, and act on rather than just think about or ponder.[10] The decision to work long hours or to save money is a value; so is the choice to be honest in filing your income tax, to refrain from sexual intercourse apart from marriage, or to drive at fifty-five miles an hour in a thirty-five zone.

When we were children, most of our values were self-centered. We did what was best for us and at times that may have included doing what pleased our parents. In adolescence there is often a period of reevaluation. Teenagers begin to question the values of their parents or the teachings of the church—especially when pressure from peers and the push for independence stimulate young minds to investigate new ideas and behaviors.

As we move to adulthood and are forced to make decisions

about life-style and careers, we have to decide what we believe in and the extent to which we will retain the values that came from our parents and teachers. Often the young adult is idealistic and accepts standards of right and wrong that are unrealistic or impossible to follow. Some throw out traditional standards and try to live a "value-free" life. Still others fail to give much thought to their values until they are presented with the opportunity to act in a way that society would consider illegal or one's parents or friends might consider immoral. At that point, one must make a spur-of-the-moment decision about behavior and values—a decision that might be regretted later. None of these alternatives is very practical as a guideline for living.

It is much more realistic to think through what you believe and the reasons for your beliefs. Then, when you are faced with an ethical dilemma, you have some standards for making a decision. Regretfully, it appears that many people never give their values this much thought, although some help may come from the ethics and values clarification courses that have sprung up recently, especially on college campuses. The goal of these programs is to help students recognize their own values. Usually there is no attempt to force people to think in a certain way and neither is there an emphasis on clinging to a rigid set of values. As the society changes, traditional and widely held values sometimes change as well, and as we grow older, most of us modify at least some of our personal standards and beliefs. In spite of this, our values tend to remain constant over life, influencing our decisions, molding our life-styles, and governing our actions. It probably is true that when people are aware of their values, they can make decisions more efficiently, change values that they don't want to retain, and prevent some of the inner turmoil that comes when two values are in conflict.

As a start in finding your values, look at how you spend your time, money, and energy. If you maintain that God is important, but skip church often and spend very little time in prayer or meditation, then it is probable that God isn't very important in your value system after all. If a young husband tells his wife their family is important to him, but then spends most of his time on projects that keep him away from home, it becomes clear that in spite of his words, the projects are more important than the family.

As you think about this, you may want to write down a list of your values. What would you write about your career, your leisure activities, your friends and family, your religion, or your willingness to accept authority? Your values might become even clearer if you could discuss the list with a friend.

It may be helpful to recognize that there can be a difference between idealized values and practical values.[11] The idealized values sound impressive. You may believe, for example, that community involvement is important, that everyone should be concerned about world hunger, or that honesty is always the best policy. But how involved are you with the community? Have you donated any money or time to help the hungry? Are you always honest? The answers to questions like these give an indication of your practical values. Idealized values salve our consciences and sometimes impress ourselves or others. Practical values guide our behavior.

Both types of values can also be changed. Many people seem to believe that one value is as good as another; that what feels right, *is* right; that values are all relative and dependent at least somewhat on the situation in which we find ourselves. Such thinking is inconsistent with the Bible. If one believes that this Book is the Word of God and that He has given guidelines for effective living, then there must be an attempt to understand and obey divine teaching. With God's help we can have lives that are guided by such clear principles as those found in the

Ten Commandments or the Sermon on the Mount. We must not steal, commit adultery, judge, gossip, or disobey the law. We must encourage one another, be loving, humble, faithful to our mates, and forgiving. The list of practical biblical values is both extensive and helpful, although it sometimes is difficult to live in accordance with these guidelines.

Even greater problems come when we encounter moral and ethical dilemmas that are not mentioned in Scripture. Does one work diligently for a dishonest employer? Is it right to leave one's family to engage in missionary service? Is it all right for a single man to masturbate? These issues are harder to resolve. Each individual must make a decision with God's help and often with the help that comes from discussion with others.

I once received a note from a young lady who was having a struggle with her parents. "They don't value what I consider important," she wrote. "Relationships with others is a good example. I think they are very important. My parents think that they are a waste of time and energy. They look down on how I spend time and it is hard for me to separate what they want for me and what I want for me—especially when I am not really sure yet what I want."

It is not easy to recognize what you value and neither is it easy to make changes. But this can be done, especially if you are able to build intimate relationships with other people.

Developing Intimacy

Erik Erikson, whose views were mentioned in chapter 1, believes that the development of intimacy is the major challenge of young adulthood.

As teenagers, most of us were concerned primarily about ourselves and our own identities. Peer pressure was powerful and it was important to know both what our friends thought and whether or not they accepted us. But we also tended to be inconsiderate, clannish, intolerant, and inclined to drop even "best friends" for no solid reasons.

All of this began to change as we grew older and started to feel more comfortable with ourselves, more aware of our values, and more willing to accept other people. As we grow into adulthood, one writer has suggested, we build human relationships that are "less anxious, less defensive, less burdened by inappropriate past reactions, more friendly, more spontaneous, more warm and more respectful."[12] As we mature, there is greater tolerance and appreciation for individual differences, often accompanied by a willingness to work at getting along with others.

The other people in our lives might be put into three groups. *Acquaintances* are people whom we know only casually. They don't know us very well and we don't know them, although we may nod or even chat informally at times. *Friends* are closer, and often spend a lot of time together. Friends care for one another, encourage one another, and usually share some similar viewpoints and values. *Intimates* are people who have all the characteristics of friends but, in addition, share their mutual concerns or inner struggles, and are psychologically vulnerable with one another. Sometimes acquaintances become friends and later an intimate relationship develops. Because of the time, effort, and risks involved, most of us can only build intimate relationships with a very few people.

There is a tendency to think that intimacy and sexuality always go together. This is true in marriage, but it should not be assumed that all intimacy involves sex. Unmarried people can develop intimacy even when they are of the same sex. Think, for example, of the intimate but nonsexual experience of Ruth and Naomi, Jesus and John, or Paul and Timothy. Young adults often discover that nonsexual, intimate relationships help to prepare them for marriage by teaching honesty, sensitivity, loyalty, and the importance of selfless giving. Intimacy apart from marriage may also be limited to certain areas of life. It is possible, for example, to be intimate with a colleague at work, but to never see this person apart from the job. Others may work together intimately on a sports team or in a church committee, but limit their intimacy to the times of their meetings.

In an insightful article published several years ago, Steven Hamon outlined eight marks of an intimate relationship.[13] These characteristics can help you determine whether or not you have intimate relationships at present, and can guide as you build intimate relationships in the future.

First, intimate friends can share openly and honestly about themselves. There is no need to impress each other or to hide weaknesses.

Second, intimate friends accept each other regardless of their circumstances or moods.

Intimate relationships involve, thirdly, a willingness to give and take. Nobody worries about who is giving more or whether one person is exploiting the other. There is true mutual support and loyalty.

At times, intimate friends share about their past lives. Often this may be close to mutual confession, but it also involves mutual understanding, acceptance, and sometimes forgiveness.

Fifth—you may like this one—intimate relationships include the freedom, at times, to show "craziness," the willingness to be silly and to laugh, without feeling that we must always make sense or act maturely if we are to be accepted.

In addition, there's accountability. Intimate friends give one another progress reports about problems, battles against sins, or struggles with undesired habits and attitudes.

Intimates also are able to disagree, talk about the disagreements, and still remain friends.

Finally, true intimacy involves a willingness to share one's friend with others. Many people cannot do that. They have a close relationship with another human, but it is neurotic because the two friends have become so close that they have withdrawn from the world. True intimacy involves what some psychologists call "nonpossessive caring."

Jonathan and David had that kind of intimacy. According to 1 Samuel 18, they were "one in spirit" and loved each other as they loved themselves. They encouraged each other, helped each other, cared, apparently shared, and persisted in their mutual devotion, even when they were separated or involved with other responsibilities. Getz has pointed out another feature of the relationship that perhaps is at the core of true intimacy.

> Though a great social chasm originally existed between these two young men (David was just a shepherd boy and Jonathan a prince), they discovered in each other a common factor that made their friendship unique. They both were men after God's heart. They both had a dynamic relationship with their Lord. And when their souls were knit together as one it was not merely another human relationship. Rather it was a friendship that was also centered in God.[14]

Intimate relationships like this are rare. More common is the high degree of loneliness among young adults.[15] When you are in a stage of transition, it is easy to feel alone and to long for close friendships, especially when it seems that all of your friends are getting married and you are still on your own. Table 3-1 gives some guidelines for handling loneliness in the young adult years.

Forming a Dream

Picture yourself ten years from now. If you had complete freedom to control your future, where would you like to be?

What would you like to be doing? What would your life be like?

The answers that you give to these questions also give an indication of what has been called the young adult Dream.[16] Levinson's research found that most young adults have a Dream. It is an imaginary image of what life could be like. At first, it is vague and unrealistic, but as one moves into one's twenties the Dream gets clearer. Sometimes the circumstances of life or the pressures of friends and parents interfere with your progress toward the Dream, but the Dream can also generate excitement, vitality, and a life purpose. Those who abandon the Dream in their twenties will find themselves struggling with this decision in later life. "Those who build a life structure around the Dream in early adulthood have a better chance for personal fulfillment, though years of struggle may be required to maintain the commitment and work toward its realization."[17]

The baby boomers were raised with the belief that Dreams can be fulfilled, and that all things are attainable through possibility thinking or a positive mental attitude. While such thinking is often unrealistic, young adulthood is a time for creative dreaming and careful planning. The issues discussed in this chapter—self-sufficiency, identity, values clarification, and intimacy—can all help you to reach greater independence and move toward the accomplishment of your Dream. According to the Yale researchers, it also helps if you can form significant relationships with other adults who will help in your progress toward the Dream. One of these adult figures is the "mentor" whom we will discuss when we consider careers. The other significant person is the marriage partner described in the next chapter.

Table 3-1
How to Handle Loneliness

Loneliness is a common experience, especially during the early adult years when there is change, mobility, and sometimes insecurity in relating to others. The following suggestions can be helpful.

1. Admit that you struggle with loneliness. If it is true that 70 percent of young adults experience some loneliness at this time in life, you are neither alone in your problem nor abnormal because you have lonely periods. To admit a need is the first step in finding a solution.

2. Ponder the possible causes of your loneliness. Are you too busy with your career? Are you shy? Do you lack social skills, struggle with a poor self-concept, or have difficulty communicating? Do other people see you as being an angry person, inconsiderate, or intolerant. Many times we are lonely because we drive people away.

3. Consider what you could do to change. You may want to talk to a counselor about your self-esteem or mannerisms. How could you learn to communicate better or to rise above your shyness? Can you juggle your work schedule so more time is available for people?

4. Look for opportunities to be with people. This may involve forcing yourself to attend church socials, to introduce yourself to people at work, to be friendly with a neighbor. Remember the old saying that the person who wants to have friends must be friendly. Remember that one of the best ways to build friendships is to offer help. The church and the community are filled with opportunities to reach out to others.

5. Resist self-pity. That is a common companion of loneliness, but it locks you into an attitude of frustration, boredom, and passivity. Can you see the bright side of life, even with its loneliness? For what can you be thankful?

6. Ask God to meet your loneliness needs. The first human need mentioned in the Bible was the need for companionship (Genesis 2:18). God, who met Adam's need, can meet yours. Ask Him to help. Follow this up by contacting a local church, perhaps meeting with the pastor, and asking where and how you can be involved with people.

7. Accept the fact that some things will not change. If you are a widow, your mate will never come back. Ask yourself how you can find fulfillment and companionship, even though your life has changed permanently.

Source Notes

1. Landon Y. Jones, *Great Expectations: America and the Baby Boom Generation* (New York: Coward, McCann, and Geoghegan, 1980), p. 1. Most of the information in the first few paragraphs of this chapter is adapted from Jones's book.

2. Alvin Toffler, *Future Shock* (New York: Random House, 1970), p. 290.

3. Daniel J. Levinson et al., *The Seasons of a Man's Life* (New York: Alfred A. Knopf, 1978), p. 75.

4. Gerard Egan and Michael A. Cowan, *Moving Into Adulthood* (Monterey, Calif.: Brooks/Cole, 1980), p. 98.

5. Levinson, op. cit., p. 74.

6. A. W. Chickering, *Education and Identity* (San Francisco: Jossey-Bass, 1969).

7. This paragraph reflects the concepts of moratorium and identity foreclosure as proposed by J. Marcia, "Development and Validation of Ego-identity Status," *Journal of Personality and Social Psychology,* vol. 3, 1966, pp. 551–559.

8. Egan and Cowan, op. cit., p. 146.

9. Candace E. Trunzo, "The Baby Boomers: Living the Good Life," *Money,* vol. 12, March 1983, p. 60.

10. S. B. Simon, L. W. Howe, and H. Kirschenbaum, *Values Clarification: A Handbook of Practical Strategies for Teachers and Students* (New York: Hart, 1972).

11. M. Rokeach, *The Nature of Human Values* (New York: The Free Press, 1973).

12. R. W. White, *Lives in Progress* (New York: Dryden Press, 1958), p. 343.

13. Steven A. Hamon, "Intimacy: Transcending Sexual Roles," *Christianity Today,* vol. 24, January 1, 1982, pp. 30–31.

14. Gene A. Getz, *David: God's Man in Faith and Failure* (Ventura, Calif.: Regal Books, 1978), p. 64.

15. Egan and Cowan, op. cit., p. 198. According to these writers, "The highest degree of loneliness is found among members of your age group (18–25). Some people estimate that 70% of the members of this age group experience loneliness as a problem at one time or another." This conclusion is adapted from L. Rubinstein, P. Shaver, and L. Peplau, "Loneliness," *Human Behavior,* vol. 2, 1979, pp. 58–65.

16. Levinson, op. cit., p. 91. Levinson and his colleagues have capitalized the *D* in *Dream* in order to "identify and emphasize" the specific and significant nature of this idea.

17. Levinson, op. cit., p. 92.

4

Becoming a Couple

Handling Your Movement Into Marriage

My friend Art has quit the ministry. I wasn't surprised when I heard the news—but I *was* sad.

During his seminary days, Art and I talked often. He was open about his struggles, excited about his future, and determined to build a life that was useful and honoring to God. When he got married, we discussed his hopes for a family and his concerns about the instability of so many marriages today. He read books about marriage, attended couples' seminars with his wife, and expressed an interest in developing skills as a marriage counselor.

One day, shortly before he left to take the pastorate of a little New England church, he asked me a difficult question. "What can I do to be sure that my marriage, which is good now, will not collapse in the future?"

I can't recall how I answered, but for some reason, I remembered that question when Art wrote to say that he was leaving the pastorate because his wife had filed for divorce.

Apparently nobody knows why modern marriages are so unstable. Psychologists, sociologists, seminar speakers, and a host of writers have given their insights about marriage instability, and there are literally thousands of books that advise couples in the principles of building a happy home. Some of these books are very insightful and practical, but it is easy to wonder if they are doing any good. The books keep being written and the marriages keep disintegrating.

In an interesting little volume, Philip Yancey once suggested that while marriage is "the most analyzed, talked about, dissected institution in this country," few people read the "facts and principles and guidelines" that are available to help struggling couples. Some of these facts are presented with confusing jargon, Yancey observed, so he decided to interview nine young couples asking them to tell in their own words how they had survived the "most dangerous" first five years of marriage.[1] Yancey's book is well written and makes enlightening reading, but even before it was published some of those "successful" marriages had begun to crumble and more than one ended in divorce.

Choosing a vocation and launching a career is a difficult challenge in young adulthood, but if you make a poor choice you can always try something new. Marriage, however, presents the Christian with a more difficult decision. The general attitude of our society seems to be that marriage partners, like careers, can be changed as one grows older, but the Bible teaches that marriage is for life. Most people who marry choose a mate in their early twenties, when several other decisions are pending and when there is a lot of uncertainty about the future. Nobody wants to make a mistake that can have implications for all of life.

Some of this anxiety was expressed by a young seminar participant who wrote, "I want to get married but this seems like a long way away and I am scared to get into a serious dating relationship." Others have expressed similar concerns, some of which might sound familiar to you:

I have trouble knowing if marriage is for me. Can I have both a career and a marriage? And how do I know who is the right partner for me? Is it okay for a younger person to marry someone older? It would be good to know God's will in my life in this specific area.

As a young adult I am trying to decide whether there is a "one and only" for me for the rest of my life. How do I find such a person? Does it take time to find out if you're compatible or do you "just know"?

I'm facing a decision between a career and a family. There is so much stress to get ahead and be a financial success, but there is also pressure to get married, especially if you are a woman. I'm aware of the fact that women outnumber men and most people my age already have families.

How do I deal honestly with another person in a dating relationship? And how do I have faith in God to provide a marriage partner for me? I have a lot of anxiety waiting for the person God intends to be my mate.

I'm already married, but how do we set up priorities in our lives? There is that conflict between intimacy and self-absorption, and it seems there is never enough time for both.

How can I understand my mate? How do we build a real partnership? Some couples seem to have it, but many do not.

One person wrote that the biggest problem in this area was deciding whether to spend most evenings praying for a mate while sitting at home isolated from other single people, or "flitting" between churches and social gatherings on a "fox hunt." "It would be easiest," this writer concluded, "if I just gave up."

To give up and forget about marriage might be an easy solution, at least for a while, but what is easiest isn't always what is best. Many people do remain single (we'll discuss that in chapter 6), but others go on to build fulfilling and lasting marriages. It may be true that marriage is "one of the biggest gambles that an individual will ever take"[2] in life, but marital success is not dependent on luck or circumstances. When a couple is committed to building a good relationship, successful marriage often results, especially when there is a willingness to seek God's guidance.

Young adults face four challenges in this area. They must learn to relate to the opposite sex, select a mate, get married, and work at building a good husband–wife relationship. Every young person faces the first of these challenges and considers the second. Those who marry are confronted by all four issues.

Getting Along With the Opposite Sex

When I was a student living in England many years ago, I decided to go to a play that was being acclaimed in the London newspapers. For seventy cents (which was all my student budget could handle) I was able to get a ticket that admitted me to what must have been the worst seat in the house. At the time I didn't realize that I was in the presence of a classic, the stage version of *My Fair Lady* with the original cast.

One of the popular songs in that production was sung by Rex Harrison, who played the role of a chauvinistic teacher and English gentleman who knew plenty about diction and grammar but nothing about women. "Why can't a woman be more like a man?" the lyrics asked. Then the singer launched into a listing of the superior qualities of the male.

Such an attitude of sexual superiority still appears in both men and women. Such people, who fail to appreciate and relate to the opposite sex, are almost certain to have impoverished lives and difficult marriages. When a young couple keeps sexual biases and relates primarily on a physical sexual basis, there is little opportunity for real understanding, communication, or the fulfilling kind of intimacy that we discussed in chapter 3.

According to the Yale researchers, the first developmental task of early adulthood is to form "adult peer relationships" with members of the opposite sex.[3] These relationships may involve affection, emotional intimacy, dependency, nurturing, friendship, collaboration, respect, admiration, commitment, and sometimes (although not always) romantic love and sexuality. Through these relationships, the young adult learns what members of the opposite sex are like, how they think, and what they find appealing.

Such opposite-sex relationships can be both good and bad. In addition to learning about the other sex, many young adults find that their opposite-sex friends are supportive, understanding, and less critical than same-sex friends. But sometimes there is misunderstanding and threat, especially when females find men who are more tender and dependent than had been expected, and males find women who are intellectually more capable than one's male friends.[4] Problems and tensions can develop if one person begins to see romantic implications in the friendship, but the other person does not. Sometimes a nonromantic, opposite-sex friendship becomes a fulfilling and time-consuming way to avoid contacts with others who might be sexually attractive. Romantic involvements can be threatening, and some people unconsciously avoid the threat by building relationships with people who are "safe" because they appear to be unlikely candidates for a marriage partner.

This leads to the issue of dating, a type of male–female relationship that has been described as a relatively recent and typically American innovation.[5] The sociological studies of dating report that most dating partners are of the same social class and family background. Emotionally stable people tend to date those who are stable; and the unstable date each other. As you might expect, couples who start dating early and see each other often, tend to marry young. People whose parents are unhappily married start dating at a younger age, marry sooner, and have difficulties in their own marriages. High school graduates who skip college and go right into work or marriage, tend to have less intellectual curiosity, less interest in new experiences, and often less stable marriages than those who take some time to "find themselves" and learn more about the world before giving serious attention to what has been called the urge to merge.[6]

Dating, of course, does not always lead to merger in a marriage. Some dates are primarily for companionship, recreation, and getting acquainted. No long-term commitment is implied or intended and the dater may be more interested in the status or convenience of having a date, than in emotional involvement. Later the relationship may become more serious, more steady, and more inclined to lead to engagement and marriage.

By the time they reach young adulthood, people in our society have had a variety of dating experiences. Some, who might not have dated during the teenage years, now feel awkward and uncomfortable as they contemplate adult dating. Others may have discovered the pleasures and dangers of becoming too involved too quickly. Such people may find difficulty in moving at a slower pace as they build adult relationships. Others may be afraid to develop new relationships because they have been hurt by dating in the past. Then there are some whose diverse dating experiences in the past have led to some personal guidelines that set the tone for more mature dating in adulthood.

Consider, for example, the experiences of Paula Rinehart. "I have experienced two kinds of dating relationships," she wrote, "one which I approached in a way typical of our generation's mentality, and one built on the firm foundation of God's principles."

The first relationship was with someone named Sam.

His first love was basketball. Sam had been a Christian from childhood and yet never elevated his hunger for God above the thrill of placing that brown ball through a hoop. In the process of our dating, though, he and his family were responsible for my conversion. Beyond that, only two things were right about our relationship: We were both Christians, and he was a guy and I was a girl.

We were regulars at church, and even occasionally discussed the sermons. But our relationship was based on the cornerstone of physical attraction, and we were each a security blanket for the other. We went through five years of the typical ups and downs marked by jealousy and selfishness. Had we not been so emotionally involved, we would have broken up much sooner.

Our parting late in our college years was painful. We both knew for months that our relationship was not what it ought to be. We were miserable with each other and just as miserable without each other. I had known Sam for so long that facing the reality of no future relationship with him was like adjusting to a divorce or his death. Closing the door on that relationship ended a chapter in my life.[7]

Later, this writer met the man who was to become her husband. Their relationship was marked by physical attraction but because there was a lack of physical involvement, they were able to focus on knowing each other's dreams, goals, and backgrounds.

My overwhelming emotion at that point was one of respect which eventually melted into genuine love.

The world knows little of this kind of love, the variety that says "I know you well—your strengths and your faults—and I accept you anyway." When we married a year later we were both convinced that God had led us together and that our relationship was the Lord's doing, and it was marvelous in our eyes.[8]

Currently, it is not fashionable to sincerely want God's leading in dating behavior or in the choice of a mate. We live in a time when premarital sex, cohabitation, trial marriages, and self-fulfillment are more valued than biblical concepts like discipline, restraint, responsibility, commitment, faithfulness, and sexual purity. Since we are molded by the society in which we live, it is easy to accept cultural ways of dating, only "to arrive on the other side of the altar with a 'ho-hum' marriage. . . . In a culture that lives for the moment and marries for the moment, the Christian's concept of lifelong commitment to one person stands out in sharp contrast."[9]

If you have spent much time in church youth groups or read Christian teenage magazines, you surely have had repeated encounters with somebody's guidelines for dating. Many of these principles are helpful, especially to teenagers who are starting to date, who are inexperienced in handling awkward sexual encounters, and who do not recognize the dangers or possible implications of seemingly innocent words and actions. Such people need reminders to date only fellow believers (2 Corinthians 6:14), to avoid circumstances that permit or encourage excessive sexual arousal, to treat each other with respect, to work on communication and getting to know one another, to pray about dating and to ask for God's guidance. Young adults could benefit from some of this advice.[10]

Unlike teenagers, however, young adults are much freer to plan their own lives and to make their own decisions about dating and marriage. It is easy to forget that each of us is sexually vulnerable and inclined, at times, to be led by our emotions and immaturities instead of by our clear thinking. The young adult who is overly anxious to get married, for example, sometimes flirts inappropriately or acts in other immature ways that may attract attention, but rarely lead to a serious and in-depth relationship. Often a friend can give some insightful perspectives on how you "come across" as you relate to members of the opposite sex.

This may not be of much comfort now, but it could be helpful to know that thousands before you have worried about their dating behavior. They have learned that dating is more common and satisfying among people who make themselves attractive both physically and intellectually, keep involved in activities and places where other single people are present (church singles' groups, volunteer organizations, educational institutions, and work settings are examples), try to keep from appearing too anxious to get married (that can "scare off" some people), and commit all of this to God, who does care about our needs and the desires of our hearts.

Selecting a Mate

Unlike societies where marriages are arranged by parents, we have a lot of freedom to determine when, if, and who we will marry. Whenever we have freedom, we also have the responsibility to make wise decisions and sometimes this creates a lot of anxiety. Most of us see the benefits of marriage: companionship, sexual intimacy, the fulfillment of our needs to be dependent, affectionate, accepted, protected, and nurtured. We recognize, too, that many people are influenced by social pressure (parents and others expect us to get married) and sometimes by the desire to get away from parents, to legitimatize a pregnancy, to find a mate who will help to advance one's career, or to prove that one is not gay. It becomes important to sort out motives and to proceed carefully into marriage if we are to avoid misery later.

One research study of two thousand couples concluded that there are five overlapping steps in courtship.[11] The first step, *initiation,* involves meeting your future mate. For you, this may already have happened; the researchers found that first meetings are usually uneventful and not noticed much at the time.

At some time you start dating. The researchers called this a *latency* stage, but it may be more accurate to call it the time of relaxed and casual dating. Friends and relatives may look on approvingly, but the couple feels uninvolved and free to drop the relationship at any time.

Eventually, there comes an awareness that this could be a serious relationship. At this *precommitment* stage, there sometimes is anxiety as one ponders whether to keep going. People who are afraid of intimacy sometimes withdraw, psychologically if not physically, and friends may make comments that either encourage or discourage the developing closeness.

Do you, as a couple, continue the relationship at this point and move on to the next two stages of *commitment* and transition to *marriage,* or do you back away? To some extent your decision will depend on how you answer three big questions.

1. *Are we ready for marriage?* According to one writer,

> a person would be ready for marriage or couplehood when he/she feels able to enter into a shared intimacy that includes sexual enjoyment and commitment; shows a capacity for tenderness and affection for the other person; displays interest in that person's emotional condition and personal adjustment; indicates a readiness to merge personal plans for the future; is willing to share economic problems and be realistic about ability to contribute to the maintenance of the joint household; and is able to delay immediate personal gratification in order to meet the needs of the other and to build the relationship.[12]

This is an impressive list, worth discussing as a couple, but you might also want to talk with a more objective friend who might give a better perspective on the extent to which you meet these standards. As you consider the issue of readiness, give some additional consideration to the idea that marriage involves some of the skills we discussed earlier.[13] In you, or in your prospective mate, is there evidence of the ability to relate to people socially, to delay getting what you want now in view of some long-term goals, to work together in solving problems or making life plans, to develop and pursue mutual interests, to coordinate a variety of commitments, to appreciate people, to be committed to others without being possessed by them, to develop self-knowledge, to understand and appreciate different cultural backgrounds, and to face and deal with disagreements? Learning in these areas probably takes a lifetime, but it is important to see where you as a couple are now, before you progress further in the relationship. Emotional highs only last for a while. The people who build good marriages are those who develop knowledge and skills in these practical areas.

2. *Are we willing to be committed to each other?* Commitment is the intellectual or emotional pledge to do something. It involves caring and taking responsibility. It is the basis of love, at the core of Christianity, and essential for a successful marriage. Commitment is also rare in our society with its emphasis on individual rights, immediate gratification, and personal achievement.

One thing about marriage is certain. There will be times of tension and disagreement. When a couple has made a commitment to the marriage and to each other there more often is a determination to resolve the problem and, subsequently, a successful resolution of the difficulty. Many marriages appear to falter because the husband and wife have been overly influenced by pressure from others or by their feelings and have never seriously considered the cost of making a commitment in marriage.

3. *Are we compatible?* To some extent, the answer to this question comes from looking at the relationship thus far. Do you have similar interests, values, and goals? Are you both committed to Christ and wanting to have Him guide your lives and marriage? Are you both open to change, willing to try new experiences, inclined to encourage, and similar in your views of issues such as the desirability of children, the spending of money, the development of dual careers, the influence of in-laws, or involvement in a church? Premarital counseling can sometimes help you consider these issues, but often such counseling comes too late—after you have already made a decision to marry, set the date, and reserved the church. There may be college or other courses that can help you consider compatibility, and several excellent workbooks, designed for couples to work through together are available at bookstores.[14]

If you are a Christian, you probably will also be struggling with God's will in your selection of a mate. *Does God want me to marry this person?* you may wonder. *Am I moving too quickly; might there be somebody better for me; if I go through with this marriage am I in danger of missing God's best for me?*

In one sense, questions like these are good. They indicate that you are not taking the prospect of marriage lightly and neither are you ignoring God's influence in your life. But questions like these can also immobilize you with fear and uncertainty, creating inner turmoil and robbing you of the joy that should be flooding your life at this special time.

In his controversial book, *Decision Making and the Will of God,* Garry Friesen argues convincingly that there is no biblical support for the idea that God has only one person for you, that He will reveal who that person is, and that your life will be miserable if you marry someone else.[15] According to scriptural teachings, marriage and singleness are both acceptable to God, and the choice of a mate is governed by only one scriptural guideline: Christians must marry Christians (1 Corinthians 7:39; 2 Corinthians 6:14–16). The implication is that you are free to choose a marriage partner, based on your own careful thinking and the thoughtful input of people who know you. The only requirement is that you marry another believer—preferably someone who is deeply committed to Christ and wanting to serve Him.

Once you make the commitment and decide to get married, you might begin to feel swept along by the expectations of your friends and parents. Showers, bachelor parties, constant talk about invitations and attendants, planning for the reception and the honeymoon—all of this becomes prominent in your life and sometimes hides the fact that, if you are like many people, the engagement period is also a time for some doubts to surface. Eloping looks more and more attractive.

Getting Married

A couple of weeks before my wife and I got married, we were surprised by a couples' shower arranged by a number of our friends. They all brought gifts, and presented us with a book of letters in which each had written some advice for a successful marriage.

One couple had a simple formula: stop thinking *me* and *mine;* start thinking *us* and *ours.* From now on it will be "our car," "our home," "our money," and "our bills." Many people might reject such advice today, only a few years after it was given, but it was helpful to us and jolted us both into a clearer awareness of the changes that were about to occur.

The move into marriage will involve "we thinking" and a variety of other changes. You will have to think differently about yourself (*I am now married, I am not as free to come and go as I once was*). Old attachments with friends and parents will have to be changed and probably loosened. New responsibilities will have to be accepted, and you will have to shift from what have been called the "self-oriented pleasures" of singleness into the "couple-oriented mutuality" of marriage.[16]

If it is planned carefully and not allowed to become an ego-boosting extravaganza, the wedding ceremony can be a meaningful time of public dedication to God and commitment to each other. Friends give their blessings and society gives its approval of your new status.

Hopefully, the honeymoon that follows will give you privacy and the freedom to relax, to discover each other at a new level of intimacy, and to experience the joys of being newly married. The honeymoon should be a time for fun, but it is best if there is plenty of time for leisure without involvement in a lot of frantic activity.

The move into marriage is sometimes viewed as the final step into adulthood; the evidence that you have at last grown up and settled down. Such thinking hides the fact that marriage involves major adjustments, including the need to throw out some of the fantasies and unrealistic expectations that most of us take to the altar.

It is easy to conclude, for example, that your love is unique, that your marriage will always be the way it was in the beginning, or that you will always resolve difficulties by calm and rational discussions. Such ideas soon change, sometimes abruptly. Old problems and tensions, hidden by the excitement of the wedding, begin to reappear. Career demands begin to exert themselves, and in-laws sometimes start a subtle or blatant interference. Assumptions that may never have been checked out ("Women always do the cooking." "Christmas will be spent with my family." "The husband is spiritual leader in the home." "Since we're Christians, we will always get along well." "We will work together in handling the household budget.") are found to be inaccurate. Soon you begin to realize that the honeymoon is over.

Building a Marriage

When the initial enthusiasm of marriage begins to fade, your thinking can move in one of two directions. You can conclude that "the thrill is gone" and that your marriage may be moving into the state of blandness or conflict that seems to be so common, or you and your spouse can recognize that your marriage is moving into a new, more realistic, and down-to-earth stage on which you can build a solid and fulfilling relationship.

H. Norman Wright has written that marriages go through stages in the same way that individuals pass through the transitions described by Erikson, Levinson, and others.[17] At the beginning, says Wright, marriages have a "season of expectations," in which the husband and wife live with high romantic intensity and only a superficial awareness of each other's needs, wants, and expectations.

Within the first year or two, the romantic idealism fades and a new stage of marriage begins to develop. Sometimes new attitudes and insecurities begin to surface, new challenges come from work or from friends and family, and there may be unanticipated financial crises or an unplanned pregnancy. Fears and frustrations often accompany these problems, and the couple must learn both how to communicate and how to deal with their anger. (These issues are considered in tables 4-1 and 4-2.) The main question of this stage is, "Will we be able to make it together?"

To make sure that the answer is yes, it could be helpful to consider the eight vital pillars that, according to Wright, form the basis of a good marriage.[18]

Goals. What are the goals for your marriage? What would you like to accomplish in the next month, year, or decade? As a couple do you have financial goals, travel goals, or goals about having children, buying a house, starting a ministry, spending regular time with each other, getting to know the neighbors, or joining a couples' Bible study?

Most of us have learned the importance of setting goals in our careers, personal finances, and education, but it is much less common for people to set goals for a marriage.

One marriage counselor has described how a minor accident disrupted his exercise schedule and left him out of shape. "I did not have to do anything to get out of shape," he wrote,

> it took no effort on my part whatsoever. When I stopped exercising it happened naturally. The same thing occurs in marriage. We don't have to do anything to get our marriage out of shape. You can take a good marriage, neglect to exercise it by not setting mutual goals or planning for fun and excitement, and the marriage will get out of shape. And you know how that once we get out of shape we invite problems into our lives.[19]

A good way to avoid these problems is for the husband and wife to each write down some short-term and long-range goals for the marriage. Try to be specific. Then plan some time to discuss these together and to merge them into mutual goals.

Expectations. As we have seen, each person enters a marriage with expectations of what marital life will be like. Sometimes the husband and wife have different expectations and in time this can lead to conflict. It is best to be open in stating and discussing your expectations. Once again, you may want to write these down prior to discussing them. The discussions (you may want to have several) can bring greater understanding and more harmony to the marriage.

Needs. We don't often think about this, but for most of us marriage meets certain needs. Some people marry because it gives security, protection, status, or the opportunity to dominate or nurture another person. More of us, perhaps, marry because we need to feel loved, to be understood, to experience sexual fulfillment, or to find companionship.

It isn't easy to recognize your needs, but it is worth trying because the better you understand your own needs and the needs of your mate, the more effective you can be in meeting each other's needs, and in turn, having your own needs met.

Handling Change and Crises.   In our hearts we know that life involves change and crises, but these are painful to contemplate, so we go through life pretending that they won't appear. When they do come, and you lose your job, have an accident, fail a college course, can't get a mortgage, or see a parent die, there is tremendous pain and discouragement. Most of us aren't prepared for this, and although change and crises sometimes pull marriages together, often they drive a wedge between the husband and wife.

Should you sit around, then, thinking of all the bad things that might happen and making plans to cope? No. But it does help to learn some general ways of coping with stress (see table 2-1) so you are better prepared when stress does appear. It also helps if you as a couple can learn to communicate and make decisions together.

Decision Making.   Who makes the decisions in your marriage? Are there some areas where you both agree that the wife will make decisions, other areas where the husband decides, and issues you decide on together?

I know a marriage where the wife makes all decisions about how the house will be decorated and when there will be guests. From what I can gather, the husband is happy with this arrangement—but it wouldn't work in our house. My wife and I enjoy decorating our home and planning our social life as a couple. If we choose to buy a chair or drapes, we don't spend the money until we find something we both like. If we decide to invite friends in for dinner we plan together. We try to respect each other's opinions in these and other decisions, and we each try not to force a personal viewpoint on the other.

Sometimes this doesn't work well in practice. I think I am usually the culprit. I tend to be impatient and want "us" to make decisions quickly, usually based on my analysis of the situation. When my wife doesn't agree, I have been known to get annoyed and impatient. I have also learned that we both feel better if we wait and work to find a course of action on which we both agree. Sometimes I have to "give in," sometimes my wife gives in, but more often we start over and find a compromise that we can both accept.

Clearly, we have formed our own approach to decision making. No doubt it is influenced by what we saw in our parents, but it has become our own way of doing things. In time, you too should work out a way to make decisions.

Conflict Resolution. This involves learning to communicate, to handle anger, and to resolve differences. Early in marriage, we will find ourselves dealing with conflict. The sooner we learn how to resolve conflicts, the better. (Please see the two tables at the end of this chapter.)

Prayer. Everybody knows that when families pray together, they tend to stay together, but even Christians seem to find this difficult. Prayer acknowledges God's presence and seeks His help with our needs and problems. It also builds intimacy in a marriage, and stimulates trust, humility, caring, mutual respect, and marital stability.[20]

Forgiveness. Recently I noticed a slogan printed on the T-shirt of a woman in the grocery store. It said, "I don't get mad, I get even."

Probably this was meant to be humorous, but in reality if this becomes a way of life, it destroys both individuals and marriages. When people determine to get even, especially in a marriage, there is certain to be continual conflict and division. Forgiveness is at the core of Christianity and surely it always is present in successful marriages. When forgiveness is absent, bitterness rises up and according to the Bible (Hebrews 12:15) and our own experience, bitterness creates all kinds of problems both within marriage and without.

How are you making progress in developing these pillars in your marriage? If you see one of the pillars crumbling, recognize that your marriage must stand on the others. If another pillar is taken away the house becomes weaker, and as other pillars erode or are found to be poorly constructed, the marriage, in time, will collapse.

I wonder if that is what happened to my friend Art? He had high hopes when he began his marriage, but it fell apart and everybody involved was hurt.

I was thinking about this recently when I happened to be reading a book written by an insightful pastor. His words might have been helpful for Art, just as they might be valuable for you:

> It takes genuine effort and persistence to establish an intimate relationship with anyone. Neither good marriages nor, for that matter, even deep friendships are made in heaven. They may be designed there, but the work of constructing them is done on earth, and only those who are willing to stay with the long-range task of faithful relationship-building will avoid the loneliness that was recognized long ago as not good for any human being.[21]

Table 4-1
How to Improve Communication

Turn to almost any book on marriage counseling and you will find that lack of communication is listed as one of the major causes of marital problems. Entire books have been written about communication in marriage, and you may want to consult some of these.[22] The following are some general guidelines.

1. Recognize that effective communication takes time, effort, and determination. If you want to communicate you will have to be willing to work at it, even when you are tired, frustrated, and don't feel like trying to communicate.

2. Listen carefully. That is the essence of communication. Sometimes we are so busy thinking of ways to defend ourselves that we don't hear what the other person is saying. Listening involves hearing the words, but it also involves paying attention to tone of voice and nonverbal clues such as facial expressions and gestures. In one study of troubled marriages, it was found that husbands, especially, did not notice their wives' nonverbal messages. This leads to misunderstanding and communication failure.

3. Express yourself clearly. Sometimes we forget this in the heat of argument. Try to express how you feel in clear, concise language without hurling charges, making sarcastic comments, or using explosive words such as *you always* or *you never.* Instead of saying, "Your stupid comments really make me mad," try something like, "When I hear comments like that I feel angry."

4. Avoid communication substitutes. Watching television, going out to work in the garden, launching into one's work, talking on the phone, or keeping the conversation at home focused on "safe" subjects like the weather, can all be ways to avoid serious discussion of tense issues. The longer you put off the discussion, the harder it will be to communicate.

5. Try to avoid communication roadblocks. These are things that get in the way of effective communication. They include interrupting each other, ridicule, putting down each other, sarcasm, and getting away from the topic under discussion. If you are having a discussion about money, for example, there is no need to bring up issues of in-laws, sex, personality conflicts, or annoying habits. Sometimes couples spend a lot of time "collecting grievances" (annoying issues that you keep in mind so you can hurl them at your spouse in the future). These grievances are then used as extra ammunition when it comes time to fight. Quit collecting grievances. If something concerns or annoys you, discuss it as soon as possible, and stick to the issue at hand.

6. Work on your communication style. Each of us has a way of communicating. When we work on showing respect, friendliness, attentiveness, openness, and a relaxed manner, we communicate better. Couples who are happily married tend to show these traits when they communicate.[23]

7. Ask God to help you communicate. Praying together is especially helpful in removing communication barriers.

Table 4-2
How to Deal With Anger

It is a fact of life that married couples get angry with each other, at least periodically. Anger occurs when we do not get what we want and/or need. Anger does not have to lead to arguments, but it must be acknowledged and expressed if a marriage is to be fulfilling and growing.

There are healthy, productive ways to handle anger and there are unhealthy, nonproductive ways. An in-depth, nine-year study of 487 couples found that happily married people consistently used the healthy–productive approach.[24] This is characterized by the following:

1. *A nondefensive attitude.* Unhappily married couples are primarily concerned with defending one's personal point of view and making sure that this point of view is expressed in no uncertain terms. Happily married couples, in contrast, listen without trying to be defensive, and they drop clues (sometimes only an "uh-huh") to let each other know that they are listening. The subtle message that is conveyed says, "I might not agree with you, but I am paying attention and working to understand what you are trying to say."

2. *An awareness of how one is communicating.* Assume a couple is having a disagreement over use of the family car. In the midst of the exchange, one person says, "You're shouting at me: you don't need to do that," or, "You're interrupting and not letting me express myself." The poor communicators will bring this into the argument ("I am not shouting; you're being too sensitive); those who handle their anger well will admit what is happening and get back to the main issue ("You're right, I was shouting and I'm sorry," or, "I didn't realize that I was interrupting, go on with what you were saying").

3. *A willingness to negotiate.* This may involve a vigorous defense of one's own position, and an admission that one is

angry, but there is also a flexibility, a respect for one's partner, and a willingness to compromise.

4. *A sensitivity to feelings.* What is your mate feeling? If you don't know, ask. What are you feeling? Your mate may help you to understand your anger. Sometimes the issues over which we disagree are covers for something more basic, such as an inability to handle stress because of fatigue or the presence of a disease, job pressures that are carried home, feelings of insecurity or helplessness. In good marriages there is an awareness of such issues and a willingness to accept and try to resolve them.

5. *An ability to resist bitterness.* Some have suggested that when a couple lets their anger turn to bitterness, it is very difficult to save the marriage. The Scriptures teach, however, that with God's help bitterness can be resisted (Hebrews 12:15); that when anger is dealt with quickly it is less harmful (Ephesians 4:26, 31); and that our minds should be filled not with thoughts of revenge and malice, but with kindness, compassion, a willingness to forgive, and a deliberate effort to think positive thoughts about others (Ephesians 2:32; Philippians 4:8).

Source Notes

1. Philip Yancey, *After the Wedding* (Waco, Tex.: Word, 1976).

2. Ledford J. Bischof, *Adult Psychology* (New York: Harper & Row, 1969), p. 61.

3. Daniel J. Levinson et al., *The Seasons of a Man's Life* (New York: Alfred A. Knopf, 1978), p. 106.

4. M. Komarovsky, *Dilemmas of Masculinity: A Study of College Youth* (New York: Norton, 1976).

5. Lillian E. Troll, *Early and Middle Adulthood* (Monterey, Calif.: Brooks/Cole, 1975). Some of the conclusions in this paragraph are based on research reported by Troll, p. 76.

6. Reported by Gail Sheehy, *Passages: Predictable Crises of Adult Life* (New York: Bantam Books, 1974), p. 103.

7. Stacy and Paula Rinehart, "Dating: Going Against the Grain of Our Culture," *Discipleship Journal,* vol. 3, January 1983, p. 41.

8. Ibid.

9. Ibid., p. 38. This article is excerpted from a book by Stacy and Paula Rinehart, *Choices: Finding God's Way in Dating, Sex, Singleness, and Marriage* (Colorado Springs: NavPress, 1982). Used by permission of NavPress, Colorado Springs, Colorado. All rights reserved.

10. One of the best available books on sex and dating is by Tim Stafford, *Love Story* (Grand Rapids: Zondervan, 1977). Although written for teenagers, this had many practical guidelines for adult dating.

11. Robert G. Ryder, John S. Kafka, and David H. Olsen, "Separating and Joining Influences in Courtship and Early Marriage," *American Journal of Orthopsychiatry,* vol. 41, April 1971, pp. 450–464.

12. Naomi Golan, *Passing Through Transitions* (New York: The Free Press, 1981), p. 67.

13. The skills listed here are adapted from Gerard Egan and Michael A. Cowan, *Moving Into Adulthood* (Monterey, Calif.: Brooks/Cole, 1980), pp. 219–235. This book includes practical exercises for evaluating and developing your competencies in each of these areas.

14. These include: Robert and Alice Fryling, *A Handbook for Engaged Couples* (Downers Grove, Ill.: InterVarsity, 1977); Joan and Richard Hunt, *Preparing for Christian Marriage* (Nashville: Abingdon, 1981); Bob Phillips, *How Can I be Sure?* (Irvine, Calif.: Harvest House, 1978); Wes Roberts and Norm Wright, *Before You Say 'I do' "* (Irvine, Calif.: Harvest House, 1978); and David A. Thompson, *A Premarital Guide for Couples* (Minneapolis: Bethany Fellowship, 1979).

15. Garry Friesen with J. Robin Maxson, *Decision Making and the Will of God: A Biblical Alternative to the Traditional View* (Portland, Ore.: Multnomah, 1980).

16. Naomi Golan, op. cit., p. 70.

17. H. Norman Wright, *Seasons of a Marriage* (Ventura, Calif.: Regal Books, 1982).

18. The following paragraphs are adapted from H. Norman Wright, *The Pillars of Marriage* (Ventura, Calif.: Regal Books, 1979).

19. Wayne Rickerson, "Goal Setting in Marriage," *Family Life Today,* vol. 9, January 1983, pp. 25–26.

20. Robert and Diane Nicholson, "Praying with Your Spouse," *Marriage and Family Living,* vol. 62, September 1980, pp. 10–13.

21. John Claypool, *Stages* (Waco, Tex.: Word, 1977), pp. 67–68.

22. See, for example, H. Norman Wright, *Communication: Key to Your Marriage* (Ventura, Calif.: Regal Books, 1974); or Joyce Huggett, *Two Into One: Relating in Christian Marriage* (Downers Grove, Ill.: InterVarsity, 1981).

23. James M. Honeycutt, Charmaine Wilson, and Christine Parker, "Effects of Sex and Degrees of Happiness on Perceived Styles of Communicating In and Out of the Marital Relationship," *Journal of Marriage and the Family,* vol. 44, 1982, pp. 395–406.

24. Anthony Brandt, "Avoiding Couple Karate," *Psychology Today,* vol. 16, 1982, pp. 38–43.

5

Becoming Parents

Handling Your Adventures in Child Rearing

Have you ever seen one of those television advertisements for disposable diapers? How easy parenthood is made to look. The babies are always clean, healthy, and cooing happily in their absorbent diapers. The parents, who change these diapers, invariably are young, attractive, slim, relaxed, and thoroughly enjoying their trouble-free little doll—with the dry bottom.

When we become parents, most of us experience these times of joyful bliss, but we soon discover that parenthood involves a lot of stress as well. Babies have a way of demanding attention without being able or inclined to give in return. They get sick at the most inconvenient times. They wake up when parents want to sleep. They cry when we want them to be quiet, and they have an uncanny ability to throw up when parents are dressed in their best clothes. Some wise person once said that if you want to know what it means to be unselfish, you should become a parent. Nothing is likely to have a greater influence on your life-style. Once you have a child, your life changes per-

manently. Perhaps it isn't surprising that in one widely reported study, 83 percent of the interviewed couples reported
that the birth of their child represented a crisis, even though
the children were planned and wanted, and even though the
marriages were considered to be stable.[1] More recent research
challenged that high percentage and showed that when a marriage is strong, couples can make smooth transitions into parenthood, in spite of all the adjustments.[2]

There was a time, not many years ago, when most young
people assumed that they would eventually "grow up, get married, and have children." People who chose to stay single or
couples who remained childless were considered unusual and
sometimes they were the brunt of unkind jokes.

All of this has now changed, mostly since the coming of age
of the baby-boom generation. Many married couples have decided to remain childless, or to delay child rearing until both
husband and wife are established in careers. The higher divorce rate has brought a dramatic increase in one-parent families. It is no longer unusual for unmarried couples to bear
children, for homosexuals to become parents or adoptive parents, or for single individuals to be involved in child rearing.
The newspapers in our community recently took delight in re-
porting that a Roman Catholic priest had legally adopted an
orphan boy as his son. Everybody in the parish was pleased;
few were surprised.

It is probable that many of these changes are good, but they
have also brought turmoil and tension, especially to young parents and their children. In the past, family activities centered
around the needs of children—perhaps too much so—but now
as a society our homes appear to have become primarily adult-
centered. Parenthood has been devalued, adult careers have
been elevated and, according to one writer,[3] the recent disturbing increase in child abuse stands as a visible monument to the

fact that many families cannot cope with the demands of child rearing. America is

> no longer a society dominated by children or even by families. As families continued to break down, more and more children were caught up in divorce and grew up with a different idea— if any idea at all—of how the traditional family operated. Many of these children are emotionally and psychologically wounded. A decade earlier, the psychiatric field of childhood depression did not exist. Now it is a growth industry. Children as young as six and seven are trying to kill themselves in numbers previously unthinkable. Yet these are the same people who will carry us through the twenty-first century.[4]

All of this can seem very theoretical until we bring it into our own lives and are faced with the questions of whether or not to have children and whether we will be able to cope if we do become parents. One seminar participant stated the struggle concisely: "Our biggest problem as a couple is to decide if we should have children in an age where the future seems so uncertain and technology appears to be outrunning people's ability to cope." The numerous books on child rearing indicate that many parents are looking for help in raising their sons and daughters. Most would agree that parenting is a marvelous experience for many people. These are the mothers and fathers who grow along with their children and enjoy the challenges of parenthood thoroughly. For others, the experience can be so traumatic that it threatens marital stability and brings parents to the breaking point.

Before thinking about ourselves as parents, it might be helpful to reflect on the attitudes of some of our friends. In pondering this, I thought of five couples whose perspectives differ radically. All of these people are Christians, and although I've tried to disguise their identities, each is very real and probably like someone you know.

We can begin with Alma and her husband. They fit the traditional-family mold perfectly. She wants to be a housewife who dotes over her husband and dedicates her time and energies to raising their three children. He is a businessman, intent on building his career, but determined not to lose his family in the process. These parents are in their late twenties, active in the church, and glad to live near both sets of grandparents.

In another part of the country, far away from their families, Don and his wife are both working, after five years of marriage. She wants to get pregnant, quit her job, and raise children. He doesn't want children and is honest enough to say why. "Children are an inconvenience," he told me recently. "They are expensive. They will interfere with my career. I suspect they will steal away my wife's attention, and to be honest, I'm not sure I can handle the demands of parenthood." At the time of their marriage, Don and his wife agreed that they would remain childless for the first five years. The time is now up, and Don is afraid to face the inevitable.

Melissa and her husband have also been married for five years. They both want children and are ready to make whatever sacrifices are involved, but Melissa can't get pregnant. The doctor hasn't been able to solve the problem, and the long process of adoption seems so discouraging and futile. In the meantime, they keep working at their jobs, keep trying to have a baby, and look with feelings of joy and sadness at their friends who are well entrenched in parenthood.

Craig is now middle-aged. He enjoys his nieces and nephews and, although we've never discussed this, I suspect he would have liked to have been a parent. But his wife doesn't like children. She has never wanted them, and even as a young adult, Craig had to accept the fact that he probably will never be a father and that he and his wife will reach old age without ever experiencing the pleasures and challenges of being parents or grandparents.

My friend Alex already is a grandparent. After his children had grown up and his wife had died, Alex decided to get married again. His new wife is a young woman who has borne two children. To put it mildly, they are a handful: active, inquisitive, noisy, demanding, and clearly more than their father can handle. He seems to be overwhelmed by the demands and, at a time when most men are thinking about retirement, Alex is immersed in his work. Is this his way to escape and to find a little peace and quiet?

Each of these couples, like each individual, is unique. How you handle parenting is likely to differ from the approaches and experiences of your friends, but four important issues face all parents. We will consider each of these in the remainder of this chapter.

The Decision to Have a Child

Not long ago I passed a man who was wearing one of those T-shirts with a slogan. "Any male can be a father," the statement read, "but it takes a real man to be a daddy."

As you well know, some couples don't think much about the responsibilities of being dads or moms until they discover that a baby is on the way. When a pregnancy is unexpected or unplanned, when a couple gets pregnant to prove that they are now adults, or when a husband and wife assume that a child will hold together a faltering marriage, the challenges of child rearing are likely to be more difficult than they will be for couples who have talked beforehand and are in agreement about their attitudes toward children.

I wonder how many people get married and don't realize, until after the wedding, that they have different ideas about the desirability, number, and influence of children? Don and his wife were like that. It wasn't until they were married that she discovered his resistance to children, and he came to realize how much she wanted to be a mother. Because this couple is willing to communicate and in view of the fact that they are concerned about each other, they probably will work out some kind of compromise. Politics isn't the only field where compromise is crucial; marriage demands compromise even more. It has been said that nothing puts more pressure on a marriage than the birth of a child. If you can talk about parenthood before the pregnancy, if you can share your differences of opinion and honestly accept your mate's viewpoints, and if you can take the time to compromise when you have different opinions, then you have made a good start to successful child rearing.

You might find it helpful to ask yourselves some difficult questions:

- What are our attitudes toward children? Do we both like them? Would we want them in our home for twenty years?
- What are the advantages of being parents?
- What are the disadvantages?
- What are our reasons for wanting or for not wanting children? Do we really want to be parents?
- When is the best time for us to start a family?
- Do we have different opinions about the desirability, number, or timing of pregnancies? How will we resolve our differences?
- Are we willing to pray for divine wisdom in our decisions about children, willing to accept God's will for our lives, and willing to have Him bring greater husband–wife unity at this important juncture of our marriage?
- What do we expect life to be like as parents? What do each of us see as "my responsibility," and what do we expect from each other?
- How do we respond to King Solomon's words in Psalms 127:3–5a?

Because of the emphasis on careers in our society, it also is important to discuss your own thoughts about the influence of children on each of your careers. Do you both plan to pursue careers outside the home? How might your children be influenced by your careers, and how will the careers be affected by children? How would you respond to the lady who wrote the following note? Does the writer say things that apply to your marriage as well as to hers?

> I'm confused about how, as a woman, I can raise a family and mix that with a career. We really want to have children and have been trying to get pregnant for more than a year without success. Even so, we're not sure we know how to nurture and guide a child if one does come along. Now I am thinking about returning to school to start my career. I am twenty-six. My husband is in seminary and I have been working as a secretary to put him through, but I don't like office work.

I wonder what will happen if this lady returns to school, starts working on that career, and discovers shortly thereafter that she is pregnant? Pregnancies have a way of appearing when they are least expected, and usually they are accompanied by a variety of emotions. These may include some (and perhaps even all) of the following: joy, excitement, depression, fear, caution, pride, jealousy, anger, anxiety, enthusiasm, embarrassment, and gratitude. In His wisdom, the Creator has given us nine months to get used to the pregnancy, to handle these emotions, and to get physically and psychologically ready for the child's arrival.

Growing Through the Pregnancy

During her first pregnancy, my wife slipped out of bed one night and moved quietly to the kitchen. I'm not sure why I woke up and noticed that she was gone but it didn't take me long to find her. Sitting at the kitchen table at three-thirty in the morning, she was joyfully consuming a plate of piping hot spaghetti.

Such was my introduction to the food cravings and other uniqueness of pregnant women. Although she never had much of a problem with morning sickness, my wife taught me about the mood swings, fatigue, tears, and clumsiness that come as a pregnancy develops. We made regular visits to the doctor for prenatal examinations, took a prospective parents' class at the local hospital, and delighted in the baby's tendency to kick my wife in the stomach—under her new maternity clothes.

Some couples move through a pregnancy with ease and confidence, especially when there is good prenatal medical care and when the husband and wife have a good relationship with each other. Even in the best of pregnancies, however, there can be fears about the baby's health, worry about finances, and concern about the mother's weight and changing physical appearance. Some couples are distressed by changes in their sexual relationship during pregnancy, and it isn't always easy to adjust to the advice from friends, the changes in life-style, and the preparations that must be made to get ready for the baby's arrival. When there are physical complications with the pregnancy, those nine months before childbirth can be especially difficult; and there can be added tensions if the pregnancy becomes the center of conflict between a couple who are having marital difficulties.

Hundreds of books are available to help couples grow through a pregnancy, and the recommendations from physicians and friends can all be helpful. Until recently, most of this advice was directed to the mother, but now there is emphasis on the father's feelings and attitudes as well.

One research study discovered, for example, that prospective fathers often go through four stages during the wife's pregnancy. First, there is the decision-making stage during which the husband must decide with his wife that they will have a child, or must accept the fact that a child is on the way. Then, surprisingly perhaps, there is a period of mourning. The father-to-be may feel sad about losing the satisfying relationship he had with his wife before pregnancy, or he may realize that in the future there will be a loss of some personal freedom. Sometimes that sadness comes when fathers unconsciously feel left out of all the activities, especially when medical people make the father feel that he is a superficial appendage to the whole pregnancy process. In time, these feelings merge into a third stage: the period of empathy. Here the father becomes very supportive of his wife and tries to help her cope. As his wife gets bigger, he may feel a sense of potency and hidden pride over his ability to get her pregnant. This does not prevent him from doing more household tasks than he might have done otherwise—all in an attempt to be helpful. Later, during the fourth stage, he begins to more fully accept the fact that the baby will be here soon, and that his life will be different.[5]

Some fathers take all of this in a casual way, attempting to remain aloof from the whole experience. Others look on the pregnancy as a burden and an interference with their responsibilities or leisure activities. Then there are those who accept the pregnancy enthusiastically and look forward to becoming "family men." As you might expect, men in the third group adjust better to children, and so do their wives.[6]

At this time in life, communication continues to be important. Because I knew that she was undergoing physical and psychological changes, I tried to shield my wife from problems during her first pregnancy. I didn't tell her about my frustrations at work, for example, even though we had talked freely about everything before the pregnancy. She wondered why I had quit talking and was afraid that I no longer loved her. We were each concerned about the other, but trying to protect each other by not communicating. Noncommunication, even for good reasons, can create tension.

I did do one thing carefully, however. We were still residents of Minnesota when our first child was born, and I lived in constant fear that we would be snowed in when it came time to go to the hospital. So every time three or four inches of snow fell, I shoveled out the driveway. Why, I wondered, did we have to have a record-high snowfall during that winter?

The Miracle of Childbirth

It is impossible to describe the emotions that accompany the birth of a healthy, normal baby. Even people who work in delivery rooms and see babies born every day, still are sobered when a woman's period of labor ends in the birth of a lively, tiny human being. One young mother, a committed Christian, called it the most moving, spiritual experience of her life. It is a time for an outpouring of praise to God.

Because of the books and courses available, many couples know what to expect at the time of labor; and because of changing hospital policies, many fathers are now able to be present in the delivery room when the baby arrives. Increasing numbers of couples even choose to have their babies at home, but if you make that decision, have some kind of plan for getting to the hospital quickly in case complications do arise.

As they wait for the child to develop during the long months of pregnancy, probably every parent hopes for a normal healthy baby, but harbors the fear that something might go wrong. Part of the joy of a healthy delivery is the relief in knowing that "everything is all right."

But what if everything *isn't* all right? What if the baby is stillborn and the expected joy becomes mourning? What if the baby experiences breathing complications or is unhealthy? What if the child is severely retarded or physically deformed?

Many physical problems, of course, can be corrected, and the child is soon on the way to leading a normal life. But nothing can be done if the baby is born dead. And severe physical abnormalities may call for immediate decisions about surgery, possible institutionalization, or complex life-support systems. All of this can create great emotional strain accompanied by grief, shock, depression, anger, and sometimes confusion. Here is a time when you need friends and family to give support and help in making decisions. Here is a time when you need a loving church and a caring pastor who can pray and give constant encouragement. Here is a time when others, including your doctor, can help you make wise decisions and avoid hasty impulsive actions that you might regret later.

At such times there is almost always guilt, much of which may be irrational. I once counseled a lady who had returned from the mission field, married, and given birth to a retarded child. She was convinced that her son's retardation was God's way of punishing her for leaving the mission field; but even she couldn't find much theological or biblical support for such a view. We cannot conclude that an unhealthy child is God's way of "getting even" with us.

How then, do we explain David's experience with a sick child? Perhaps you remember that King David once had an affair and when the woman got pregnant, the king tried to hide his actions by arranging for the death of her husband. Clearly, David had sinned and he must have felt some guilt when the baby became very sick shortly after birth. For seven days the father "pleaded with God for the child." David fasted, lay prostrate on the ground, and refused to eat. When the child died, the servants were afraid to tell the king lest he "do something desperate."

But when he heard the news, David got up, washed, changed his clothes, ate, and went to worship God. The servants were amazed, but David explained his actions. "While the child was still alive I fasted and wept. I thought, 'Who knows? The Lord may be gracious to me and let the child live.' But now that he is dead, why should I fast? Can I bring him back again? I will go to him, but he will not return to me."

David knew that God does not hold grudges. When He forgives, He does not follow this with punishment, even though we sometimes have to live with the consequences of our actions, just as David had to live with his grief. When the child died, therefore, David worshiped God, even in his grief. Recognizing that he would see the child again someday, the king went to comfort his wife, and before long they had another child.[7]

The Challenge of Child Rearing

Once a healthy child is born, your life changes forever. At first, everything is exciting and fun. The mother is still tired from the delivery, but strength begins to return soon, and the new parents may be buoyed by feelings of relief, well-being, pride, and even euphoria. Presents, cards, and messages of congratulations start to arrive, and there often are friends and relatives who come to give encouragement and practical help while the new mother gets back on her feet.

It doesn't take long for the young parents to discover, however, that this new little relative can be extremely demanding. It is true that babies smile and coo and cuddle, much to the pleasure and amusement of their admiring parents, but babies also vomit, need to be changed, cry for long periods without stopping, and wake up at all hours of the day and night. Even when fathers do their best to help, young mothers often struggle with sleeplessness, loneliness, and sense of inadequacy, feelings of frustration, and what one counselor has called a constant struggle between gratification and desperation. Some new mothers "move about in a chronic fog of fatigue and lack of sleep, while they struggle to keep up with the round-the-clock schedule at a time when they are still recovering from the physical drains of pregnancy and childbirth."[8] Often there is a *postpartum depression*—that sense of discouragement which undoubtedly has physical causes, but also comes when one feels incompetent. Sometimes a woman will feel helpless, lethargic, unable to concentrate, and angry toward both the baby and her husband. If the baby is colicky or especially demanding, even the most gentle and loving parents can find that their patience and forbearance begin to wear thin.

For some people, all of these demands stimulate marital tension or lead to frustration-caused outbursts of violent child abuse. Others discover that the pressures of parenthood bring forth a new level of tolerance, giving, and maturity that had not been seen previously. Child psychologists have noticed that this is the time when a bond often develops between mother and child—sometimes to the chagrin of the father, who begins to feel left out and jealous.

For the new parents, this is a time for adjustments in three areas. First, the parents must learn to adjust to the child. This includes learning something about child care and how to figure out what's wrong whenever the baby cries. Second, the couple must learn new ways of adjusting to each other. No longer are they a family of two. They are now a threesome and that sometimes is difficult to handle. Third, there must be new adjustments to the outside world. How do we handle in-laws who want to give advice? What do we do about a social life that now has to be restricted, even if there is money for baby-sitters? What happens now to the wife's career? What changes need to be made in shopping routines, housecleaning, or what now may be seen as the "new challenge" of getting everybody ready and out to church? How do we handle the incredible, and perhaps unexpected, costs of being a parent—especially when we discover what doctors charge or that those cute, little baby outfits that are too small after a month nevertheless cost almost as much as adult clothing? Once again, communication, sensitivity, and a willingness to give all become important. It helps too if you can learn to handle discouragement and burnout, perhaps using some of the skills summarized in tables 5-1 and 5-2.

If you talk to other parents, including your own, you'll probably discover that almost everyone will agree on at least three conclusions about child rearing:

1. *It is not easy to be a parent.* The demands are great, but so are the rewards. Perhaps there is no experience in life that can do more to help us mature as adults.

2. *All parents feel inadequate, at least periodically.* Isn't it sobering that God, in His infinite wisdom, gives the responsibilities of child rearing to people who are young and inexperienced? And, in spite of our insecurities, most of us "pull through" and see our children grow to adulthood.

3. *We all make mistakes.* No parent is perfect and, as our teenage children will freely proclaim, none of us is infallible. But in spite of our failures, the children do grow up and usually develop into mature adults. This is a cause for gratitude to God, and it should encourage parents of all ages to pray for wisdom in their child-rearing activities. God does not expect any of us to be perfect. Our responsibility is to seek His guidance and to do the best job we can in raising our sons and daughters.

The Stages of Parenthood

Earlier in this book, we talked about stages through which all of us pass as we move through life. Probably you won't be surprised to learn that, in addition to these stages of life, it has also been suggested that there are stages of parenthood.

According to Ellen Galinsky, who wrote a book about this, there are six stages of parenthood.[9] The first of these, *the image-making stage,* comes before the child is born. During pregnancy, expectant parents think about how their lives will be changing, ponder what their baby will be like, mull over ways in which the husband–wife relationship might be altered, wonder what kind of parents they will be, and talk over their plans for the future, now that a first child (or an additional child) is on the way. Later, the new parents probably will discover that some of these early plans and images were unrealistic, but the act of thinking about the future and talking about it, helps couples get ready for the baby's birth and eases the transition into parenthood.

The second period of parenthood, *the nurturing stage,* goes from birth until the child starts to say no, usually between eighteen and twenty-four months. This is the time of initial adjustment to the new baby. Couples discover what it really is like to be parents, and as the months pass, they become attached to the child and get to know him or her better.

The parents also get to know themselves better. They see their own weaknesses, insecurities, and unrealistic expectations. "I was going to be a perfect parent," one young father wrote. [I was going to be] "loving, caring, nurturing, soft. I was going to make up for all the men who leave children to the women, who back away from intimacy with children, who are cold and distant. I was going to do it right. Tonight I see how scared I am. There is so much to do for this little creature who screams and wriggles and needs and doesn't know what he needs and relies on me to figure it all out. . . . I need to accept my fear, my reluctance, my instinct to flee. I have to start from where I am."[10] That involves being realistic and not trying to live up to our own or some other person's image of the ideal parent.

In the nurturing stage, parents must also learn to make new

adjustments to each other, to grandparents, to other parents, and to older children if there are any. Sometimes there is the pain of realizing that childless couples, who once were good friends, now seem distant, not especially interested in children, and clearly unable to appreciate the demands or restrictions that parenthood puts on you. Sadly, you realize that old bonds of friendship are fading.

All of this leads parents to question their priorities. What is this baby doing to our lives? How is this child changing us? How much time and attention should I give to this baby and how much should be given to the other aspects of my life?

Even as you work on these issues (and sometimes start the process all over again with the arrival of another child), you move into *the authority stage*. By this time the child is approaching his or her second birthday, and for the next two or three years parents must make decisions about rules. What are the rules? Who enforces them? What happens when they are resisted and broken? How do we deal with power struggles? How do we respond when grandparents or neighbors make observations about our failures or give advice about how we can be more consistent parents?

This is the time when many parents begin looking for books on discipline. If we didn't know it before, we begin to see that parenting really is a skill; one for which few of us have had much prior training. We struggle with the reality of our failures and inconsistencies; we grapple to find a balance between time alone or as a couple versus the demands of this little person who is teaching us that the "terrible twos" is more than a catchy slogan.

This is also a time when most of us delight in the discoveries that the child is making. We try to answer a stream of questions, deal with incessant requests, arbitrate in disputes with other children, and experience those marvelous days when we visit the zoo or circus with our kids.

When the child enters school, we begin *the interpretive stage,* which lasts until the beginning of adolescence. As this period begins, we who are parents tend to reflect on our child rearing thus far. We begin to wonder whether we should change some of our approaches. Have we taught the values and attitudes that we want our children to have? How do we want our children to behave in school, at home, with their friends? How will we teach independence without giving them too much freedom? How will we answer their questions, teach them to be realistic, or interpret the world to them? Most of us don't anticipate all of these issues before they arise. More often they come upon us without warning and demand an immediate response. When a child asks how women get pregnant, for example, or wonders why God lets little children die, there is no time for the parent to ponder his or her theory of sex education or theology of suffering.

If you are a young adult, just getting started as a parent, you probably have little interest right now in Galinsky's two final stages: *the interdependent stage,* when your children will move through the teenage years, or *the departure stage,* when they leave home to build their own families and careers. When your children are in their twenties, I suspect you will find that the stages of parenthood do not end when our offspring leave the nest. Good parents try not to meddle in the lives of their adult children, but neither is it possible or desirable to stop being a mother or father as soon as our youngest leaves home. The stages of parenthood probably continue until we reach the end of life and sometimes make the discovery that our children are "parenting" us.

As you think about your present stage of parenthood, it might be good to ponder three sources of practical help that many parents find useful.

1. *Reading is helpful.* There are literally thousands of articles and hundreds of books dealing with parenthood. Some of

these can be very useful, especially when they point out that your problems are not unique and that your children, with all of their demands and frustrating ways of acting, are more normal than you thought.

The problem with books and articles is that they don't always agree with one another, they often seem unrealistic and idealistic, and at times they are intimidating with their advice about how you should act as a parent. No one author has all the answers and neither is any writer consistently right. Books (including this one) are best seen as sources of help that need to be evaluated and pondered without being accepted uncritically. You are the one who must raise your children. With God's help, you are the one who tries to do as well as you can in child rearing. If a book can give help, that may make your task a little easier.

The bookstore salesperson can often recommend helpful things to read and so can your friends. You might also notice advertisements and book reviews in magazines, but in the end we each make our own decisions both about what to read and about whether the author's conclusions are useful.

2. *Other people can be helpful.* In former times, young parents were surrounded with grandparents, aunts and uncles, cousins, longtime neighbors, and a variety of other parents who could give advice and encouragement when it was needed. In our present age of mobility, many of us are far away from relatives. There are advantages to this independence, but there is also the disadvantage of having no relative to turn to in times of need or uncertainty.

This does not mean that there is nobody to help. The people in your church, the members of your Bible study group, the women in your neighborhood "young moms' club," or some older couple in your apartment building can all give guidance when you need it. In raising our children, my wife and I have often talked informally to parents with children just three or four years older than ours. Often these more experienced parents can give fresh perspectives on our child rearing, and we in turn have been able to do the same with parents whose children are a few years younger than ours.

As your children get older, don't overlook the rich source of help that can come from school. You may have one troublesome seven-year-old to handle, but the second-grade teacher has a whole classroom full of these little people, and often that teacher can give a perspective you had never considered.

Parenthood is most difficult when we try to do it without help. Most of us live in communities with other people, many of whom have experienced the challenges that we are facing now. It makes sense to use this valuable and available source of help and information.

3. *Finally, prayer can be helpful.* It would be more accurate to state that prayer is essential. Each parent needs wisdom from above and Christian parents are in special need of divine guidance as we seek to bring up our children, not only to become responsible, mature adults, but to be followers of Jesus Christ who have been raised "in the training and instruction of the Lord" (Ephesians 6:4).

The Bible is filled with guidelines for living, but it doesn't say very much about child rearing. There is one verse about child rearing in Ephesians, for example, one in Colossians,[11] and a few scattered proverbs about the training of children. Deuteronomy 6 gives one of the most complete statements, when God instructs the Israelites to love the Lord, to obey Him, and to teach His commandments to children at every opportunity.

Clearly, parents have a responsibility to teach spiritual truths to their children. Perhaps this is best done, not only by what you say to your children, but by the Christian life that you live. It is sobering to ponder this, but parents are the best examples of mature human beings that their children see. Your marriage is a model that your children notice. And the best example of a Christian is you. As they get older, children see other models, but the example of their parents makes an indelible impression.

Child rearing can be challenging and a lot of fun. But parenting is also a serious business—best handled by prayer.

Table 5-1
How to Cope With Discouragement

Parents aren't the only people who get discouraged. At times we all feel "down," often we don't know why, and frequently we seem unable to pull ourselves (or others) out of the emotional doldrums.

The following suggestions could be helpful, but one caution should be kept in mind: Discouragement, especially the persistent sadness and sense of futility that signals depression, often has a physical cause. If your discouragement persists, it is important to seek professional help. The following are guidelines to think about when you feel the periodic "blueness" that comes into all of our lives.

1. Accept the fact that everyone gets discouraged. Even the greatest of biblical saints got discouraged at times, and you will too. Don't accept the old hymn phrase that we should "never be discouraged" if we are people who pray. Discouragement is a part of living. It certainly is a part of parenting.

2. Don't try to fight the discouragement. This doesn't usually work. Telling yourself or someone else to "cheer up and stop being discouraged" often makes matters worse.

3. Try to determine what is making you discouraged. If you can find the cause, you can take steps to try to deal with the cause and to change the situation. There can be a variety of causes. The following questions can help you think of what might be causing your discouragement.

- Have I been getting enough sleep?
- Have I been getting exercise?
- Have I been eating a balanced diet?
- Is there some other physical problem that might be influencing me psychologically?
- Has something happened to hurt me? What is it?

- Am I angry about something? What is it?
- Have I lost something: a friendship, a relative who has died, an opportunity, a job, my health?
- Do I feel helpless about some situation?
- Have I let myself slip into a pattern of negative thinking?
- Is there some other stress in my life?
- Is there unconfessed sin in my life?
- Do I feel guilty about something?
- Have I let myself become bitter?

4. Ponder what you might do to remove the cause of your discouragement. If you can't think of solutions, a friend can often help you get a better perspective on your situation.

5. Try to talk to yourself realistically. *Is the situation really as bad as it looks? Is my perspective too limited? Am I worrying about things that probably won't happen? Can I do anything to change my attitudes?* Ponder Philippians 4:8; then apply it.

6. Stay involved with people. It is natural to withdraw when we feel down, but this pushes us further into our discouragement. Try to keep in contact with others. If this is difficult, ask someone to prod you a little so you stay involved. The support and encouragement of others is something everybody needs.

7. Take a look at your environment. Dark rooms, depressing pictures, and "heavy music" can all pull us down. Try to brighten the places where you live and work.

8. Become a people-helper. Reaching out to others who have needs can do wonders to perk you up—but try not to get involved with other discouraged people or you risk pulling each other down. If you don't know how to be helpful, ask your pastor for suggestions.

9. Remember that prayer changes things. Make it a habit to read the Bible every day and to ask God to help, even though you don't feel like praying or reading Scripture.

10. If things don't get better, get some help. Sometimes a

friend can give the help you need. At times a pastoral counselor will be helpful. At other times you may need to seek
professional assistance.

Table 5-2
How to Deal With Burnout

Burnout refers to a feeling of physical, emotional, and mental exhaustion. It comes after one has had prolonged involvement with people or work situations that demand time, energy, and strength.

The term *burnout* was first used to describe counselors, physicians, and other professionals who become tense, discouraged, and worn-out as a result of working with demanding people. More recently, *burnout* has been used to describe policemen, business people, pastors, and any others who wear out because of their involvement with people. Research has shown that college students are especially prone to burnout, and that burnout can occur both because of marital tensions and because of the pressures of demanding children.[12]

1. Learn to recognize burnout symptoms. These include: physical exhaustion, sometimes accompanied by an inability to sleep; emotional exhaustion as seen in persisting discouragement, feelings of helplessness, impatience with people, low morale, self-pity, and a "what's the use" attitude; and mental exhaustion including self-condemnation, forgetfulness, a hypercritical attitude, bitterness, lowered productivity, and a lessened ability to concentrate.

2. Ask yourself if you feel helpless, run-down, and bored. These are common characteristics of burnout.

3. Make up your mind that you will find a way to get away from the pressures, at least periodically. This, of course, is not easy, but it may be the only way to survive. Even Jesus pulled away from the crowds, and you need to get away at times from the children or the job pressures. Sometimes this only involves a couple of hours when somebody else can "cover" your responsibilities while you take a mini-retreat.

4. Keep alert mentally. If boredom is a problem, do some-

thing to occupy your mind or to give you a diversion from routine responsibilities. In one family with small children, the father used to come home at night and read to the mother while she finished household chores. This gave her some intellectual input and adult interaction after a day of talking to preschoolers.

5. Find a support group. Even if you are burned-out because of the demands of people, you still need others. But find a friend, church group, or family member who can give support and encouragement without making a lot of demands.

6. Ponder what, if anything, can be done to remove the causes of the burnout. One study of parents found, for example, that burnout was highly likely when parents put excessively high demands on themselves to be perfect and always patient, were isolated from other people who could give support, were bored, and were confused about how to handle child-rearing problems. Can you think of ways to deal with such issues?

7. Pray about your burnout. Christ has promised to give peace (John 15:1, 27; Philippians 4:6, 7) and we can pray that He will not only help us through our time of burnout, but bring us into contact with others who can give practical support when we need it.

Source Notes

1. E. E. LeMasters, "Parenthood in Crisis," *Marriage and Family Living,* vol. 19, 1957, pp. 352–355.

2. For a brief summary of this research, please see Naomi Golan, *Passing Through Transitions* (New York: The Free Press, 1981), pp. 80–81.

3. Landon Y. Jones, *Great Expectations* (New York: Coward, McCann & Geoghegan, 1980), p. 212.

4. Ibid., pp. 216–217.

5. Laurence Barnhill, Gerald Rubenstein, and Neil Rocklin, "From Generation to Generation: Fathers-to-Be in Transition," *Family Coordinator,* vol. 28, 1979, pp. 229–236.

6. Lucie Jessner, Edith Weigert, and James L. Foy, "Development of Parental Attitudes During Pregnancy," in *Parenthood: Its Psychology and Psychopathology,* ed. J. E. Anthony and T. Benedek (Boston: Little, Brown, 1970), pp. 209–244.

7. The account of this incident is found in 2 Samuel 12: 1–25.

8. Golan, op. cit., p. 94.

9. Ellen Galinsky, *Between Generations: The Six Stages of Parenthood* (New York: Times Books, 1981).

10. David Steinberg, *Fatherjournal: Five Years of Awakening to Fatherhood* (New York: Times Change, 1977), pp. 13–14.

11. Ephesians 6:4; Colossians 3:20.

12. Ayala M. Pines and Elliot Aronson, with Ditsa Kafry, *Burnout: From Tedium to Personal Growth* (New York: The Free Press, 1981), pp. 170–172, 178, 180.

6

Becoming a Single Adult

*Handling Your Adjustment to Singleness,
Divorce, and Widowhood*

Have you ever looked back over the years and considered
how unexpected events often change the course of our lives?

After leaving graduate school, I expected to be a professional counselor and perhaps a professor. It never occurred to
me that I would write books, and even more remote was the
idea of teaching in a theological school. When a seminary president once asked me to join his faculty, I rejected the idea on
the spot. But the idea had been implanted in my mind and five
years later I accepted another invitation, wondering even then
if this was a respectable place for a psychologist to work.

Most of the time it has been a "fun place" to work, but there
have been times of sadness. Several years ago, for example, we
lost two of our students during the same academic quarter.
One of these young men (they were both in their twenties, both
married, and both named Paul) used to get up before dawn
each day, slip out of his apartment, and drive to the freight
company where he worked for several hours loading trucks
before the start of classes. One morning a drunken driver, returning from a party, swerved around a corner, hit Paul's car
head-on, and killed him instantly. When his grief-stricken wife

woke up their two little girls that day, she told them that their daddy had not gone to work. He had gone, instead, to heaven.

The other Paul knew that the end was coming. He fought his cancer and endured the pain with a tenacity and gentleness that we all admired, but in the end he lost the battle. The saddened campus community gathered for the second memorial service of that academic year.

Death is never easy to face, but somehow it seems harder when a young life ends. Unless we have lost a child of our own, probably none of us can really understand the pain of parental grief. Until a mate dies, we really can't feel the emptiness that comes with widowhood. Who would have predicted that the wives of these two students would be forced to cope with widowhood even before they reached the age of twenty-five? Because it happens so rarely, most young adults don't think much about facing terminal illness in themselves or adjusting to the death of a spouse.

We do think about divorce though. That is how an increasing number of young marriages end—even marriages that began with great expectations. When a couple separates, there is always pain, grief, frustration, a sense of failure, and the stress of having to readjust to one's changed status in life.

Do you think adjustment to divorce is easier than adjustment to widowhood? Would the changes have been harder to accept if those two students wives had lost their husbands through divorce? Who knows? One writer has suggested that loss through death tends to be more intense, but loss due to divorce is more bitter.[1] One lady whose first husband died and whose second marriage ended in divorce, wrote a book about her experience and gave it an insightful title: *By Death or Divorce . . . It Hurts to Lose*[2]—either way.

It can also hurt to never be married. One of my former students graduated from seminary with high grades and good recommendations. He wanted to enter the ministry and appeared to be eminently qualified. He was deeply spiritual, active in his local church, an exceptionally good preacher, socially at ease, handsome, and always neatly dressed.

He was also single.

"I'm only twenty-four," he told me one day, after several fruitless months of trying to find a job. "Sure I want to get married, and someday I probably will, but in the meantime, people don't trust me. They try to line me up with their daughters, they joke about my bachelorhood, and they tell me that nobody wants an unmarried pastor."

Judging from the singles I know, if my friend doesn't find a wife these problems could get worse. If you are a person who reaches thirty without getting married, people begin to wonder what's wrong. You must be too demanding, some assume. Perhaps you're scared of the opposite sex, afraid to leave your mother, not mature enough to settle down, or homosexual. Rarely do people say this to you directly, but the attitude is common in our society: It isn't okay to be single.

It also isn't easy to be single. I've seen this in the notes that people hand to me whenever I speak at a singles' conference. Consider these, for example:

> I have a great struggle with self-worth. I'm still young, but I am bothered by my past failures and mistakes—and it isn't easy to be a single parent.

> Can my life be fulfilling if I continue to remain single longer than I thought or wanted?

> I have trouble knowing how I, as a single, fit into a world where, if you're not a couple, you don't (and aren't allowed to) fit in socially, spiritually, and employment wise. I go to a singles' class at church, but that doesn't help much. Doesn't anybody know that singles are people too?

I'm twenty-one with two small children and no education to support them decently. My former husband is not following through on divorce promises—like money.

My major stress is not being able to understand, meet, or talk to others on anything other than work issues. Not having good interpersonal relationships for several years makes you unaware of how to meet, talk, and develop a relationship. Sometimes you can't even look at people because you're afraid of what they might or might not say. When you do make friends, you realize how much you're hurting so it's better, after a while, to not even try.

Since my wife died, I'm not sure how I fit into society. The friends we had as a couple seem awkward when I'm around. I don't fit very well with the college-age crowd, but it's not easy to be alone after several years of marriage.

I've got one problem: men. You can't live with them and you can't live without them.

The Bright Side of Singleness

One of my single friends (who admits that she would like to be married, but recognizes that she probably will stay "forever single") recently made a comment that is worth pondering: "It's better to be single and wish you were married, than to be married and wish you were single."

In thinking about never-married and formerly married people, it is easy to focus on problems without giving much thought to the positive side of singleness. There are advantages to being single, even if you hope some day to be married or re-married.

The Apostle Paul was a single adult who clearly favored marriage but who once wrote an interesting essay in which he argued that while marriage can be good, singleness can be better.[3]

He suggested, for example, that single people have a *freedom* that is unique. "Some days I come home very tired and think how good it is that I don't have to cook dinner for someone else and be charming and witty," one businesswoman wrote. She is also freer to come and go when she wants and is able to devote more time to her work if she is building a career.

Of course, there isn't much freedom if you are a single parent who has to work at a job and raise a family at home, both without the support of a mate. Probably there are days when, as a single person, you would gladly give up some of your freedom in exchange for companionship, for someone with whom to share your hopes or struggles, and for sexual intimacy.

In his biblical essay, Paul recognized this need for intimacy, but he also knew marriage creates pressures and concerns that many single people are able to avoid. The New Testament was written at a time when the world was in crisis—just as it is now—and Paul reminded his readers that it is possible to be so concerned about marital struggles, security, safety, and possessions, that there is little time left to be interested in God and spiritual issues. Marriage creates pressures and demands that single people are free to avoid.

Singleness also gives a unique opportunity for *service.* The married person, writes Paul, is concerned about pleasing his or her family, but the single person is able to devote more time and energy to serving Christ. While applauding the people who take family responsibilities seriously, Paul's letter to the Corinthians is especially supportive of those unmarried people who choose to "live in a right way in undivided devotion to the Lord." How sad that there are people like my seminary student friend who are eager and willing to devote extra attention to Christian service but who are rejected by church members, most of whom may be sincere but who don't want and won't trust single people to be in positions of leadership. How easy it is to forget that Jesus and Paul were both unmarried, and better able to serve because they were without family responsibilities.

Were Jesus and Paul also fulfilled and happy? It would be difficult to argue that something was lacking in their lives because they were single. On the contrary, Paul argues that single people have a unique *happiness* which married people lack—especially those married people who wish they were single again.

None of this is intended to deny the loneliness, rejection, low self-esteem, sexual frustration, and depression that exists in abundance among the millions of single adults who work and live, often alone, in our society.[4] But these problems are found as well among married people, many of whom are trapped in miserable marriages and lacking some of the privileges that come to single adults.

The Crisis of Divorce

Divorce is always stressful, not only for the couple involved, but for their children, their parents, and often for their friends. Most people marry when they are young, and since most divorces occur within the first seven years of marriage,[5] we can conclude that divorce is a problem that especially involves young adults. There was a time when most of us went to weddings and assumed the smiling couple would live "happily ever after," but now we know that many of those happy relationships will disintegrate into miserable marriages, painful separations, and personally devastating divorces, all while the husband and wife are under thirty.

Why is this happening? The answers are legion. Lack of commitment, inability to communicate, pressure from jobs, interference from relatives, disillusionment with marriage, self-

centered attitudes, the widespread emphasis on personal pleasure and fulfillment, the de-emphasis on sexual and marital fi-
delity, unwillingness to compromise, failure to heed biblical
teachings—these and numerous other reasons have been proposed, while literally hundreds of self-help books and seminars
have been produced in an attempt to strengthen marriages and
prevent divorce. But the high divorce rate persists, and things
don't seem to be getting better. Why?

Getting along with people is a skill that involves a lifetime of
learning. Getting along with a mate demands more than interpersonal skills, such as those summarized in table 6-1; there
must also be a commitment to one's spouse and to the sanctity
and permanence of marriage. At a time when people don't
know how to get along, divorce is widely accepted, the Scriptures are ignored or explained away, and termination of a
marriage "for incompatibilities" is an easy way to escape from
a difficult situation, it seems unlikely that we will see a renewed
willingness or ability of people to commit themselves to the
work of making their marriages last and grow. Perhaps the
people who read all of those books and attend those seminars
are the people who are most committed to working on their
marriages—and least in need of the self-help aids.

It probably will not surprise you to learn that specialists in
counseling and family life have proposed several lists of stages
through which couples pass as they divorce. One writer, for
example, suggested that divorce is so similar to grief that the
stages are basically the same: a time of denial, followed by
overlapping phases of loss and depression, anger and ambiva-
lence, reorientation of life-style and identity, and eventual acceptance and readjustment.[6] Someone else has suggested that
divorce has several aspects including legal, emotional, economic, and psychological transitions.[7] None of this is of much
practical value unless it helps you to better understand both

how people move toward divorce and how you or others can avoid divorce.

To help with this understanding, let us consider four stages of divorce, with some characteristics that you might see at each phase.[8]

Disenchantment.   Long before there is even any thought about divorce the stage of *disenchantment* begins. Maybe this is typical of most marriages. The early enthusiasms wane, the couple becomes more aware of their differences, and it becomes clear that getting along won't always be easy.

The disenchantment is often so subtle and slow that it isn't recognized at first. For example, one or both of the partners may begin to withdraw. There is more involvement in work and in taking care of the house or children. Often, less time is available for being together, there are fewer social contacts with other couples, and there may be changes in personal grooming. If a couple is committed to the marriage and able to communicate, they can talk about these subtle changes as soon as they notice them. Often this is enough to stop the withdrawal and to remind the husband and/or wife that they need to spend more quality time together.

In contrast, the process of disenchantment is speeded up if one partner begins to grow, perhaps as a result of personal study or career promotion, and the spouse remains the same or resists any change. Major life stresses—such as an unexpected illness, loss of a job, death of a relative, an unwanted pregnancy, or a physical injury—can also stimulate marital tension, and so can a shifting of values. When one person changes religions, for example, problems often arise, and there is also disenchantment if the husband or wife begins to think differently about issues such as the role of women in society, the value of children, the importance of money, or even the sanctity of marriage. When these changes begin at home and are not discussed or resolved, the spouses begin to compare their marriage with others that seem more desirable, and sometimes there is a "looking around" at members of the opposite sex who seem more attractive then one's mate.

If the disenchantment continues, one or both of the mates begins to ponder privately whether the marriage will survive. Sometimes there is self-blame, disappointment, vacillation in one's view of the marriage, fault finding, feelings of apprehension and uncertainty, discouragement, and a wondering whether or not separation is inevitable. In time each mate tends to become defensive, sad, angry, and sometimes inclined to make snap judgments that may have little basis in fact but become the fodder to feed overt arguments or mental suspicions.

Separation Decision. Eventually, the couple arrives at the *separation decision* stage. Separately or together the husband and wife begin to weigh their alternatives and to ponder whether or not they should separate.

Sometimes the decision is not mutual. One person concludes privately that the marriage is over, begins to make a mental list of what is wrong with the mate, and looks for an opportunity to "drop" the decision to separate, along with all of the grievances that have been collected in preparation for this announcement.

Even when the idea has not been presented in this unexpected way, a decision to separate is never easy. Often there is vacillation, at times there are doubts about the wisdom of this move, and frequently there is a searching for support from friends or relatives who are likely to give their approval. (People who aren't likely to approve are usually told later, after the decision to separate is harder to revoke.)

Transition.   The *transition* stage involves action. The decision to separate has been made, and the time has come to take the legal, economic, and geographical moves that break up the household.

The emotions at this time can be diverse, contradictory, and overwhelming. Joy, relief, sadness, anger, guilt, fear, feelings of failure and rejection, insecurity—all of these and more can sweep over the couple, even when both are in favor of the divorce.

Practical questions are of special importance at this time. Is this a trial separation or divorce? Should we get or continue counseling? How do I tell my friends? How do I handle finances, relate to the children, respond to in-laws, deal with my attitudes toward divorce and remarriage, cope with my loneliness and sexual urges, or make ends meet financially? Support and practical help from family and friends are important at this crisis time, but often this support is lacking when you need it most. Other people don't always understand or approve of your decision to separate and sometimes they are more critical than caring.

Readjustment.   The final stage, *readjustment* may be long and difficult. One survey found that most divorced people are determined to recover from the separation and trying to cope with their stresses.[9] They do this in several ways: by social activities, such as the development of new friendships; by becoming more independent; by involvement in home and family activities, such as taking care of the house or devoting more time to the children; by the new learning that comes from counseling or from a return to school; by expressing feelings; and by pondering what went wrong so that future mistakes can be avoided. The people who showed the best recovery and reached a high level of "postdivorce life satisfaction" were those who focused on the first three of these techniques—social activities, the development of independence, and involvement in family activities.

Separation and divorce, like the death of a mate, are grief experiences. In time the pain will pass, but recovery is often slow, and some scars of separation remain forever. If you are divorcing, you need the loving support of friends; if you are the friend, your care and encouragement can have a powerful impact in the life of someone who is in need. And you are likely to learn some things that will prevent divorce in your own life.

The Crisis of Widowhood

When I first began teaching, one of the students in our college was a young man named Lindon Karo. I only remember him vaguely, but after graduation he went to seminary and eventually became pastor of a Baptist church not far from the college in Minnesota. He loved to preach and once decided to give a series of messages on the apostle's creed.

But the series was never finished. Lindon Karo was stricken with a rare type of bone cancer that took him through a prolonged illness and led to his death at age thirty-two. Left with three active young boys, his widow, Nancy, still found the time to write *Adventure in Dying,* a moving account of her husband's last days.[10] I read it again before writing these paragraphs and concluded what I have long felt: There are no words that can convey the pain and sadness of dying and grieving.

A few years before Lindon Karo's death, a psychiatrist named Elisabeth Kübler-Ross suggested that dying people and their families pass through five overlapping stages.[11] Many people have heard of these: the stages of denial, anger, bargaining, depression, and finally acceptance. Physicians and counselors have debated about whether everyone encounters these stages,[12] and some have suggested that strong religious beliefs help people to face death more courageously.

Nobody denies that death hurts, however, and everyone

agrees that widowhood can be especially difficult. Most people are over fifty before they lose a mate, and for this reason the professional writing about grief tends to focus on older people. Many of them are comforted by their adult children, but often there are fears about the future and insecurity about the ability to readjust, to build new relationships, or to move through old age alone.

The younger widow or widower is less concerned about old age, and young people tend to have greater flexibility. But there are no older children to bring comfort, same-age friends don't always understand, and grieving in-laws sometimes add pressures. Also, the grief may be intensified by the responsibility of raising children who need special attention and understanding at a time when it is hardest to give. Even if you are widowed young, you probably will agree with those older people who maintain that one never "gets over" the death of a mate even though you learn in time to live with the loss. This is true even when you have caring friends to give support and a close relationship with Jesus Christ who brings comfort in times of mourning.

Adjusting to the loss of a mate takes time. At the beginning there is likely to be shock, a state of numbness, and an inability to "take in" the news, even when it was expected. The presence of friends and relatives brings support, the prayers of fellow believers bring comfort, and the funeral preparations may keep the spouse busy during these first hours of mourning. The full impact of the loss may not hit until later, after you have had a little time to recover from the original shock.

Within days after the funeral, the numbness begins to wear away and the reality of the death begins to register. Deep sadness, crying, guilt, yearning, self-blame for things that didn't get said or done—all are mixed with the increasing awareness that the spouse is gone permanently. Separation anxiety becomes a reality as the surviving mate faces the challenges of coping alone.

Often there is disorganization, forgetfulness, inefficiency, sleeplessness, deep feelings of loneliness, and sometimes an inability to think clearly or to communicate effectively. If ever there is a need for spiritual strength and support from accepting friends, this is the time. Going through clothes, looking at mementos, making decisions about the future, dealing with feelings of apathy and depression, and picking up the responsibilities of daily living can all be physically and emotionally draining.

There is evidence that this period of mourning can also bring growth, a greater self-awareness, spiritual maturing, and a new sensitivity to the pain of others, but the widow or widower is unlikely to see these benefits at the time. More often, there is an acute awareness of the aching void in one's life—a void that stings with special impact on anniversaries. The deceased person's birthday, for example, the first Christmas or wedding anniversary following the funeral, or the first anniversary of the death can all seem to open the slowly healing wounds and bring a fresh onslaught of grief.

In time, of course, that wound heals over, even though it probably will leave some deep scars. There has been time to rethink the past, to adjust to the reality of the present, and to turn one's attention to the future. For some, there will be a need for counseling to help with the readjustment. For everyone, there is a need for friends who show love and give both help and companionship.

Eventually there also may be a greater ability to see the death in clearer perspective. Following Lindon Karo's death, one of his friends remembered the words of an older man. "Death at a young age seems tragic to us now," he stated, "but from the vantage point of a hundred years hence—or from eternity—we'll realize that it is not how *long* we live but how *well* we live that matters."[13] That is a sobering thought for those of us who still are alive and healthy.

The Challenge of Recovery

Several years ago a psychologist, a psychiatrist, and a poet combined their talents to write a simple little book on how to survive the loss of a love.[14] The main suggestions, some of which are included as a part of table 6-2, focused on the emotional wounds that must heal if one is to overcome not only separation, divorce, and death, but other losses such as the breakup of an engagement, the failure of one's health, or the loss of a job, home, or cherished friendship.

Each of these losses involves both intense feelings and the need to make practical decisions. The mate who is left alone following a divorce or death, for example, must often cope with relatives, learn to live alone or as head of a single-parent family, struggle with finances, face the issue of remarriage, make vocational readjustments, build new friendships, and make realistic plans for the future.

Several months before Lindon Karo learned of his cancer, another young pastor was facing a different kind of crisis. One day, without much warning, his wife announced that she had never loved him, that she was filing for divorce, and that she would be taking their two children and moving twenty-five hundred miles away to her hometown in Ohio. She added that her husband would be the big loser. He would lose his family, his marriage, his career as a pastor—everything. Within weeks his family was gone, along with his pastorate and most of his self-confidence.[15] Abruptly, this man was faced with the sense of loss, feelings of inadequacy, confusion, depression, and insecurities that are so common after a marriage ends.

As a divorced minister, he could no longer serve as a pastor in his denomination. He was considered a failure and a "wash-out," who would have to forsake his training for some other kind of work. The intense pain, he reported, was like a three-hundred-pound weight on his shoulders, but he concluded that he somehow had to rebuild his life. He determined to accept what could not be changed, and resisted his natural tendencies to withdraw from people, to wallow in self-pity, or to spend time mentally blaming others or himself for what had happened. Realizing that God never stops forgiving, guiding, and loving, the young divorced pastor began to seek divine guidance for his future. Could he still have a ministry that would honor God, serve people, and bring out the best in himself? Slowly he saw God heal and bring a new usefulness and fulfillment to a broken life.

Perhaps one of the most amazing chapters in the Bible is Hebrews 11, where we find a list of the great men and women of faith. Some of these remarkable people overcame tremendous difficulties and achieved greatness because of their faith, but other equally dedicated believers were tortured, starved, ridiculed, and murdered. Life, it seems, isn't fair—at least while we are on this planet; but our task as believers is not to judge or to burrow into bitterness. God calls us to resist the sin and harmful attitudes that entangle us, to decide that we will both seek and do God's will, and to keep thinking about Jesus, who understands our pain because of the suffering in His own life. If we "consider him," we read in the Bible, we "will not grow weary and lose heart."[16] We can pick up life and start rebuilding, even when the past has been difficult.

The Bible tells us that God cares and is with us, but it never promises that life will be easy. It can be difficult to handle emotions, to resist self-defeating attitudes, to make wise decisions about the future, and to persist in our actions. It is hard to keep going when there is no mate to back us up or few friends to help us keep things in perspective. Sometimes our parents or other well-meaning people add confusion by questioning the wisdom of our plans and decisions.

It probably is wise to follow the old advice about not making major decisions too quickly after a marriage ends. If possible, allow some time for careful deliberation, make sure you pray about your decisions, and find at least one person who can give you an outsider's perspective before you act.

We need this help when we cope with career decisions, major financial expenditures, and changes in our living arrangements. If you are a single parent you will likely need support even more.

Divorce and death have a way of creating havoc in surviving families. Like their parents, children also grieve, but often they don't know how to express their hurts, insecurities, sadness, and fears about the future. Some children become demanding, manipulative, and rebellious, often in an unconscious attempt to find the new limits and to see if they are still loved. Because you feel sorry for the children it is easy to shower them with attention and presents; because you feel angry about their insensitivity and constant demands, it is hard to remain patient or to control your tongue. With divine help and some support or periodic advice from your married and single friends, try to create a homelife that is as "normal" as possible. That involves communication, understanding, spiritual teaching, shared responsibilities, discipline, and love.

As you build your one-parent family, try also to think of all four grandparents, if they are still alive. With so much emphasis on the bereaved or divorcing spouses, and on the needs of children, we sometimes forget the pain that parents feel when they see their adult children lose a mate. How will your former in-laws relate to you and to their grandchildren now? How do your own parents respond? As a single adult, you probably have enough to handle without the additional worry about your parents. They may want to help, even to the point of interference, and you may have to assert your own independence. But try to look at your situation from their point of view. Think of how they must feel. And remember that parents can be a source of encouragement and support, especially if you are sensitive to their needs during these difficult times of crisis and readjustment.

During my years of teaching, I have noticed two kinds of student reactions whenever we discuss singleness. Some students have concise intellectual theories about how to help, what advice to give, and who might be at fault. In contrast, another group is more sensitive, caring, forgiving, and understanding. The people in both groups are committed Christians who seek to be guided by biblical teachings; but while one group is rigid and insensitive, the other is compassionate and understanding. There is no doubt in my mind who will make the better counselors.

Most of us understand better if we know someone who has lost a mate or has struggled with singleness. If you are unmarried, remember that some people will understand you and be able to give help or encouragement; others won't. If you have friends who are single, remember that the most helpful person in their lives might not be a professional counselor. The greatest help may come from you.

Table 6-1
Getting Along With People

Whether you are old or young, single or married, it isn't easy to get along with people. Little children want their own needs met immediately and they don't know how to wait, to give, or to compromise. As we grow older, we learn how to cooperate, how to communicate, and how to develop interpersonal skills.

When your skills don't seem to be working, you might ask yourself the following questions. Notice that these can apply to marital tensions, but they are not limited to one kind of problem. They are questions that could be asked whenever there is difficulty in getting along with people.

1. *To what extent am I committed to Christ?* In 1 Corinthians 3:1–3 we read that interpersonal tension is a characteristic of nonbelievers and of Christians who are spiritually immature. When we are committed to Christ and wanting to be led by the Holy Spirit, we begin to show the love, joy, peace, patience, and self-control that help us get along with others (Galatians 5:22, 23). If you aren't getting along, perhaps you are trying to bring peace as a result of your own efforts. The starting point for good relationships is a commitment to Christ.

2. *To what extent am I the problem?* Do you remember the story of the man who couldn't see clearly to criticize others because there was so much wrong in his own life (Matthew 7:1–5)? Are there attitudes and actions in your life that may be accentuating the problem? Be especially alert to bitterness (Hebrews 12:15).

3. *To what extent is my tongue the problem?* It is easy to criticize, argue, gossip, and put down people verbally. All of this creates tension but never helps to cool things down. James 3:2–10 is worth reading frequently.

4. *To what extent is dishonesty a problem?* Within recent

years there has been great debate about the value of honesty. Obviously we can be so honest that we hurt people; but we can also hold back what we are thinking in such a way that people are misled and harmed. Be honest with God about your interpersonal tensions, be honest with yourself, and then seek to be honest with others, always seeking to speak the truth in a loving way.

5. *To what extent is misperception a problem?* Everyone has had the experience of jumping to conclusions about some issue, only to discover later that the conclusions were wrong. Before you criticize or even think unkind thoughts, make sure that your facts are accurate. If another person appears to have wronged you, go to that person to discuss the issue. If you appear to have been misunderstood, try to bring clarification. If you don't understand somebody else's position, ask for more information. You may find that the other person has some misperceptions too. He or she may not know your point of view.

6. *To what extent is poor communication a problem?* This overlaps with the previous paragraph. How often do people criticize and argue, without trying first to talk rationally in an effort to reach a mutual understanding or compromise? How can you do this?

7. *To what extent is permanent tension a problem?* In Romans 12:18 we read, "If it is possible, as far as it depends on you, live at peace with everyone." Is the writer implying that there are times when it isn't possible to live in peace with other human beings? What can you do if the other person is stubborn, bitter, unwilling to communicate, and not willing to understand your position? When this happens, keep working to bring peace, but recognize that some interpersonal tensions may take a long time to get better, if at all.

Table 6-2
How to Survive the Loss of a Love

The above title is taken from a book published several years ago.[17] We experience the "loss of a love" when a mate dies or when we go through a divorce, but there are other losses that can be difficult to handle.

The children of a broken marriage experience the loss of a parent and sometimes the loss of a home, both at the same time. Your parents may be struggling with the loss of a son-in-law or daughter-in-law. The death of a child, parent, or close friend is certainly a loss, but the pain of separation also comes when close friends move, our children leave home, a respected colleague retires, some loved one loses his or her health or mental stability, an engagement breaks up, or we leave college roommates following graduation. Each of these losses is painful. Each might be helped by the following suggestions.

1. Admit your loss. The sooner you face the reality the better.

2. Recognize that some losses may be permanent. Death, of course, is irreversible; other losses may be temporary, but try to be realistic in your thinking and not deceived by unrealistic hope.

3. Realize that people often pass through stages as they adjust to a loss. There is shock, denial, anger, discouragement, and eventual acceptance. Realize that such a process is normal.

4. Admit that it hurts. To pretend that you don't hurt is a way of fooling yourself and prolonging the pain.

5. Realize that healing takes time. There will be periods of progress and times of apparent regress, but remember this: You *will* get better.

6. Take care of yourself physically. It might be hard to sleep and you may not want to eat, but try not to let your body get run-down.

7. Don't let yourself slip into bitterness, blaming, and self-pity. There will be times when these appear in spite of your best efforts, but ask God to keep you from wallowing in these.

8. Try to see things from a positive perspective. Philippians 4:8 is an important verse that should be applied frequently.

9. Develop an attitude of thankfulness. What can you be thankful for? Hans Selye, the famous expert on stress, once wrote that the most harmful human attitude is resentment; the most therapeutic is gratitude. Can you be thankful, even in the midst of your pain? Look at 1 Thessalonians 5:18.

10. Keep active. You might not feel like it, but activity and involvement with the community keeps you growing and alert, intellectually and as a person.

11. Try not to make major decisions, at least for a while. When you have lost a love, your judgment is not always clear, and you are in danger of making decisions that you might regret later. Remember too that you are vulnerable right now, and some people might try to take advantage of you. If you do plan to make a decision, check first to get the perspective of a friend whom you trust.

12. Recognize your need for human contact. Accept the comfort and support of others. If such help does not come, seek it. If you don't know where to start, make an appointment to see a pastor and get some suggestions. We need other people if healing is to occur.

13. Recognize your need for God. Jesus Christ loves us, cares for us, and comforts. Ask Him to bring peace into your life, and pray that He will sustain you and guide.

14. Surround yourself with brightness. This may seem unimportant, but there is evidence that your attitude is brighter when you live in bright rooms, are surrounded by bright pictures and living plants, or listen to nondepressing music. If your bedroom is painted gray or blue, consider changing to a brighter, lighter color.

15. Recognize that some emotions are common and may keep reappearing. Anger, sadness, depression, anxiety, lack of

confidence, low self-esteem—all of these can be accepted as normal, then ask God to help you conquer them.

16. Consider keeping a journal. This need not be anything fancy, but it can help you to work out your tensions; and later you can look back and see how much you have changed.

17. Try to develop some new interests and new friendships. You won't be able to do this at first, but when you are stronger this can help the healing process.

18. Be a people-helper. At the beginning you may not have much strength to give, but in time you will learn that helping others, even in small ways, is a good way to help yourself.

19. Start making some plans for the future. As you begin to feel better, ask what you can do with your life from this point on. Try to find activities that honor God, help others, and make use of your God-given gifts and abilities.

20. Never forget the nearness of God (Philippians 4:5b). Keep reminding yourself what He is like: loving, compassionate, wise, powerful, forgiving, just, and sovereign. If you have trouble believing this at times, ask Him to help you. Take time every day to read the Bible, even when you don't feel like it. This teaches you about God and brings comfort.

Source Notes

1. Barbara M. Newman and Philip R. Newman, *Understanding Adulthood* (New York: Holt, Rinehart and Winston, 1983), p. 307.

2. Amy Ross Young, *By Death or by Divorce . . . It Hurts to Lose* (Denver: Accent Books, 1976).

3. You can read Paul's essay in 1 Corinthians 7:24–40.

4. "Nineteen Million Singles: Their Joys and Frustrations," *U.S. News & World Report,* February 21, 1983, pp. 53–56.

5. In 1962, one research study (T. P. Monahan, "When Married Couples Part: Statistical Trends and Relationships in the Divorced," *American Sociological Review,* vol. 27, 1962, pp. 625–633) reported that most separations occur within the first year of marriage and that most divorces occur within the first three years. A more recent report (M. Hunt and B. Hunt, *The Divorce Experience* [New York: McGraw-Hill, 1977]) indicated that most divorces occur within the first seven years. Only about 12 percent of divorcing males are over forty; 14 percent of divorcing females are age forty-five or above.

6. Reva S. Wiseman, "Crisis Theory and the Process of Divorce," *Social Casework,* vol. 56, 1975, pp. 205–212.

7. Paul Bohannan, "The Six Stations of Divorce," in *Divorce and After,* ed. Paul Bohannan (Garden City, N.Y.: Doubleday Anchor Books, 1971).

8. These stages are adapted from suggestions given by Naomi Golan, *Passing Through Transitions* (New York: The Free Press, 1981); and Nathan W. Turner, "Divorce in Mid-Life: Clinical Implications and Applications," in *Mid-Life: Developmental and Clinical Issues,* ed. William H. Norman and Thomas J. Scaramella (New York: Brunner/Mazel, 1980), pp. 149–177.

9. W. H. Berman and D. C. Turk, "Adaptation to Divorce: Problems and Coping Strategies," *Journal of Marriage and the Family,* vol. 43, 1981, pp. 179–189.

10. Nancy Karo with Alvera Mikelsen, *Adventure in Dying* (Chicago: Moody Press, 1976).

11. Elisabeth Kübler-Ross, *On Death and Dying* (New York: Macmillan, 1969).

12. There are several theories about the stages of mourning. The following paragraphs are adapted from C. Murray Parkes, *Bereavement: Studies of Grief in Adult Life* (New York: International Universities Press, 1972).

13. Karo and Mikelsen, op. cit., p. 9.

14. Melba Colgrove, Harold H. Bloomfield, and Peter McWilliams, *How to Survive the Loss of a Love* (New York: Bantam, 1976).

15. This pastor tells his story in Dale E. Galloway's *Dream a New Dream: How to Rebuild a Broken Life* (Wheaton, Ill.: Tyndale, 1975).

16. Hebrews 12:3; also see vv. 14, 15.

17. Colgrove et al., op. cit. Some of the conclusions in this book have been adapted into table 6-2.

7

Becoming a Career Builder

Handling Your Goals and Vocation

Have you ever wondered how your life has been affected by television?

If you were weaned on "Sesame Street" or if "Mr. Rogers" was one of your first baby-sitters, you probably have difficulty imagining what growing up must have been like when radio was king, when television was still in the future, and when nobody had heard of video tape recorders. How different is life in the present when twenty-four-hour television is available to almost everyone, and when a flick of the switch can bring news, sermons, movies, cultural performances, comedy, or pornography into the privacy of our own homes. All of this is now taken for granted. For the first time in history, a generation of young adults has been raised on television.

Nobody really knows how much this modern invention has influenced our thinking and molded our values. Numerous research studies show that television has stimulated violence, gobbled up time, and produced a generation characterized by social awkwardness, poor verbal skills, a reduced ability to concentrate, and a reluctance to read. As they passively watch their television screens, millions of people are indoctrinated into believing that all problems can be solved—often quickly and easily, that divorce is normal, that drinking is a part of the good life, that old people are eccentric or inept, that authority is not to be taken seriously, that we can have what we want, and that true happiness comes with fame or money.

Television has been criticized frequently, and sometimes unfairly, but most of us probably would agree that "the tube" exploits people commercially and paints a picture of life that is unreal and often unchristian. Rarely does the television screen even allude to a philosophy that warns us, "Watch out! Be on your guard against all kinds of greed; a man's life does not consist in the abundance of his possessions" (Luke 12:15).

Jesus never talked about job satisfaction or vocational fringe benefits. He criticized those who exploited others to get ahead, who were driven by the lust for power and success, who misused people commercially, and who valued prestige and affluent consumption more than a humble commitment to God. The teachings of Jesus and the images of television appear to be in vivid contrast; a contrast so sharp that it cannot be ignored by people who want both to grow spiritually and to succeed in their careers.

Getting established in a career is one of the biggest challenges of the young adult years. It is a challenge fraught with excitement and frustration, success and disappointing failures. It is a task that might be helped if you remember several basic truisms.

First, life is not easy. This has been called "a great truth, one of the greatest truths,"[1] but most of us don't believe it, at least until we reach middle age. Instead, we complain about problems, try to avoid them or find someone else to solve them, and live with the assumption that life should be easy—as it so often is on television. Such an attitude fails to recognize that "it is in the whole process of meeting and solving problems that life has its meaning. . . . It is only because of problems that we grow mentally and spiritually."[2]

Second, it helps to remember that life isn't always fair. Most of us would like to believe otherwise, but as we grow older we realize that some people get ahead through dishonesty, that hard work doesn't always pay off in this world, and that *who you know* is sometimes more important than *what you know.* Armed with these facts, we are not free to be dishonest or sloppy in our work, but a lot of frustration can be avoided if we recognize that there is injustice on this planet, and that sometimes you and I are its victims. It also can be helpful to read Psalm 73 periodically.

Third, realize that there is limited room at the top. This has always been true, but in recent years, the baby-boom population has swelled both the labor force and the numbers of people competing for a few places of leadership in the business and professional worlds. A generation that grew up expecting success and the good life, is finding that only a few "make it." The philosophy of certain success through positive mental attitude, is leaving thousands frustrated when confronted with the hard realities of life.

Fourth, would you agree that everybody can be successful? Much depends on how we define *success.* In our society, power, prestige, and possessions are the major marks of success, and the life goals for a lot of people. But for many of us, influence and affluence never come and in themselves they rarely bring happiness. If you want to be great, Jesus told His disciples, you should seek to serve others (Matthew 20:25–27). Christ Himself had one purpose in life—to do the Father's will (Hebrews 10:7). He never became rich, but He was successful because His main goal in life was obedience to God.

All of this may sound theoretical, discouraging, and not very practical—especially as we seek to grow in our careers. There is nothing wrong with having high aspirations or wanting to do a good job in our vocations, but the Christian must keep aware of the biblical teachings about work. That is both realistic and practical.

Our vocations influence a lot more than the hours we work or the amount of money we earn. Where we live, the people we have as friends, our life-styles, how we spend our leisure time, even our marriage partner or place of worship can be influenced by the job. For the young adult, then, it is important to find an occupation and launch a career. If you are like many of your friends, you might make one or several vocational changes before settling into a more permanent line of work. You will also be deciding about extra education, learning more about your interests or abilities, and facing the tensions of on-the-job training.

Many people have no choice but to move into whatever work is available. Your career is likely to be more satisfying, however, if you can plan ahead and choose your occupation before starting to build a career.

Finding an Occupation

Have you even wondered how your grandparents chose their lines of work? It has been suggested that people in the past reached their late teens or early twenties, made a relatively firm decision based on family expectations or available opportunities, settled into their life work without much further thought, and stayed there until retirement. In many parts of the world, this is still how job decisions are made.

Finding an occupation is not that simple for us. Most people think about their life work for a long time, and many of us struggle for several years to sort out our interests, abilities, goals, preferences, and opportunities. We start exploring different job possibilities almost from childhood and continue through the high school years. In college, we often take a variety of introductory courses and settle at some time on a major.

The nonstudent often tries several jobs before focusing on a more specific line of work.

As a result of this exploration, we begin to discover the benefits and disadvantages of different kinds of work. We begin to see where we might fit and are able to reject a number of vocations for which we clearly are not suited. Our real interests and abilities become clearer, and we are faced with the realization that most of the fulfilling and rewarding jobs require a period of training. For some people, all of this exploration is done casually, without much planning or thought. For others there is vacillation, and a willingness to let circumstances direct their careers. Then there are those who try to plan their careers more rationally, giving thought to their own abilities and exploring the world of work more systematically.[3]

If you are a more systematic planner, you might want to write down answers to the following questions. Ask a friend who knows you well to look over your answers and to give his or her opinion about what you wrote.

- What are my major areas of interest?
- What are my gifts and special abilities?
- What do I want in a vocation: fulfillment, a good income, travel, an opportunity to help others, contact with people, good fringe benefits, a place to use my talents, a place to serve God in a special way, prestige, opportunity for advancement, etc.? List your preferences in their order of importance.
- What kinds of work can best fit with my abilities and desires?
- What training would I need to enter my preferred line of work? (If you don't know, where could you get this information? Could your local library help?)
- What opportunities are available? Am I looking at an overcrowded career field, or at a vocation that is open to only a few people who have special education or abilities?

- What do my parents and close friends think about my choice of work? Do I agree with their assessment? Why?
- If I could plan my life, what kind of a person would I be and what work would I like to be doing ten years from today?

As you answer these questions, you probably will realize that your values, motives, past experiences, talents, beliefs, insecurities, hopes, personality traits, goals, and life Dream (if you have one) can all have an influence on your choice of career. The Christian, however, has another issue to consider: What does God want me to do with my life?

In a lengthy and award-winning book, Edith Schaeffer wrote how she and her husband had seen God guide as they developed L'Abri, their spiritual center in the Swiss Alps, and as they each entered a worldwide ministry of speaking and writing. In one place she wrote:

We had been living by prayer in a very vivid way, trusting the Lord to show us literally hour by hour what to do, where to go, and to provide the means. . . . But we *couldn't* have been clever enough to organize all that fell into place so quickly as we started to pray for God to unfold His will, as well as to send the people of His choice to us, and to supply the material needs. We were asking one basic thing, that this work would be a demonstration of God's existence. . . .

What were our "visions" or "expectations" or "goals"? Simply a desire to demonstrate the existence of God by our lives and our work. . . . God is very patient and gentle with His children, as in a real measure . . . they attempt to live in close communication with Him, asking for help, asking for strength, depending on His wisdom and power rather than on their own cleverness and zip! . . .

We continued to live moment by moment, having things to be thankful for, things to rejoice about with excitement, things to regret and ask forgiveness for. We wept, we laughed, we thrilled, we agonized, we squealed with surprise. Reality is not a flat plateau. . . .

We especially asked that *our* lives would be a demonstration of *His* existence, in some small way, and not of *our* own strength.[4]

Within recent years there has been a lot of talk about management by objectives. People are encouraged to set goals for their lives or businesses and to work step by step toward the attainment of these goals. Dr. Ted Engstrom, a dedicated Christian who heads a large and influential missionary organization, has outlined principles for setting goals, establishing priorities, and planning one's career. Some of these principles are included in table 7-1. Each can be helpful as we move to bring our vocational dreams to reality.

But the Schaeffers didn't build L'Abri using these principles. Instead of management by objectives, they chose to let God lead while they sought divine guidance over every decision in their lives and work. Their example surely is a challenge to anyone who seeks to make decisions—including vocational decisions—that are consistent with God's will. Do we wait for divine leading, "trusting the Lord to show us literally hour by hour what to do . . . asking for help, asking for strength, depending on his wisdom and power" rather than on our "own cleverness and zip"?[5] Do we set priorities and work toward them? Can we do both?

Surely, like the Schaeffers, we should seek to honor God in everything we do, trusting Him to guide in our lives. At the same time, again like the Schaeffers, we can use our God-given brains to make decisions that are consistent both with biblical teaching and with good principles of logic. It would be wrong, for example, to work in a career that stimulates immorality, takes advantage of people, or is characterized by deception and dishonesty. These are clearly inconsistent with biblical teaching. But there are many "honest" careers, where we can honor Christ by our competence and diligence, and where we can use our minds to set priorities and to make the best possible decisions about the future.

A former student once sent me a note that expressed a common dilemma. "I have received two excellent job offers," he wrote. "After weighing all (and I do mean all) the facts, and seeking counsel, I have decided that all the pros and cons balance out equally. My feelings don't seem to lead either way, and after a lot of prayer, I don't feel any sense of direction. How do I make a decision?"

In all seriousness, I suggested that this man could flip a coin, start moving in one direction, and assume that God would make it clear if He wanted something different. Apparently both of the alternatives were desirable and neither conflicted with scriptural teaching. At a time like this, we can trust God to lead, ask Him to guide, and then make decisions based on the available evidence and on our best thinking. In His wisdom, God did not make human beings to be nonthinking robots. He gave us minds to be used and when we want to serve Him, He will lead, whether we sense this or not.

Building a Career

One person has defined a career as "a succession of related jobs, arranged in a hierarchy of prestige, through which persons move in an ordered (more-or-less predictable) sequence."[6] This formal sounding statement expresses what most of us have seen, maybe even in ourselves: a common tendency, during a lifetime, for people to change jobs periodically, with the hope that each new position will be better than the one before.

Once we have found some suitable employment, it is easy to "get into the rut" of going to work, doing the minimum that is required, collecting our paychecks at week's end, and going home to more interesting activities. Such an attitude does nothing to advance our careers and neither does it honor Christ. "Whatever you do," the Bible tells us, "work at it with all your heart, as working for the Lord, not for men.... It is the Lord Christ you are serving" (Colossians 3:23, 24).

The more diligent worker strives to do a good job and gives some thought to career management. This involves making an effort to get along with others at work, learning to cooperate with superiors, improving one's skills or knowledge, and working toward personal and vocational goals.

The longer you remain in the work force, the harder it is to make career shifts. One survey found that 42 percent of the people questioned felt trapped in their jobs and unable to move to something as good or better.[7] At times most of us feel frustrated with our work, and it isn't easy to stay at a job where we are not appreciated. When we are young, however, it is a little easier to make a move. You have fewer fringe benefits to give up if you move, fewer family responsibilities to keep you in one place, and more job opportunities. Even society looks on with acceptance and often approval if you pull up stakes once or several times during your twenties and move into something new.

According to Dr. Daniel Levinson and his research colleagues at Yale, this career building (even with the moves) can be greatly helped if you find a "mentor" to guide you into the world of work.[8] A mentor is someone, usually a few years older, who has greater experience and seniority in the field of work that you are entering. Although a mentor can be a stranger who is admired from a distance, most mentors are people we know, perhaps eight to fifteen years older than us, who are willing to spend time guiding us into our careers.

The ideal mentor should act as a teacher who helps the younger person learn skills and acquire useful information, a model who serves as an example of someone who is already in the field, a counselor who gives encouragement and moral support, a sponsor who helps another get introduced to the occupation, and a guide who initiates the protége into the customs, language, values, ethics, and people in the field. If you can find a good mentor, your entrance into a career is made a lot smoother.

However, mentors sometimes get threatened by the emerging competence of their protégés. There is a weakening of the strong, positive feelings and even love that once existed, and in time there may even be some competition. Bitterness and anger sometimes follow, but this doesn't have to happen. As you find your place in the field, you are less in need of a mentor. If he or she can then let go and encourage you to grow on your own, you will have a friend who is now a peer, and one to whom you can always remain grateful.

As you work with your mentor and grow into your career, you probably will make some initial decisions about an issue facing Christians who are involved in career building: the question of success. We have been described as "a nation of individuals relentlessly pursuing success."[9] This pursuit drives millions in quest of the status, money, and power that we discussed earlier in this chapter.

There is nothing wrong with being successful in one's field. It is an admirable goal to be competent in our work, to do the best job possible. The problem comes when our whole lives are geared toward avoiding failure, being recognized, and driving to get ahead.

For some reason, many people have concluded that only those who succeed are really worthwhile people. We have difficulty separating who we are from what we have accomplished.

If we fail in our work we assume that we are failures as people—even though the Creator declared that His creatures are valuable regardless of our success or failure at work.

This drive for success is costly. Hundreds of magazine articles have described the ulcer-prone, stress-dominated lives of workaholics, but many keep driving nevertheless. In some occupations there is little freedom to do otherwise. But when work dominates our lives and consumes our thinking it becomes a god. When possessions become too important, we can succumb to the love of money that is described in the Bible as the root of all evil (1 Timothy 6:10). We can forget that it is God "who richly provides us with everything for our enjoyment" and commands us "to do good, to be rich in good deeds, and to be generous and willing to share" (1 Timothy 6:17, 18). Prestige and acclaim, if they become important, can lead to pride and even create insecurity as we struggle to squelch our competitors and to stay at the top of our fields.

Several years ago a delightful little book appeared, describing the story of a caterpillar who discovered a pile of other caterpillars all squirming and pushing to climb a big caterpillar tower. The hero of this story joined the climb, stepping on other caterpillars and pushing to get to the top. When he got there he found nothing, although he spotted a few butterflies that seemed beautiful and free of the mass of caterpillars struggling to knock each other off the pedestal. Disappointed, the caterpillar hero went down from the pile, eventually spun a cocoon, and in time became the butterfly that it was meant to be.[10]

This simple yet profound book has sold thousands of copies, perhaps because it is so relevant. In the climb to get ahead, we can cease to be what God intended and instead find ourselves pushing other human beings aside in our struggle to get to the top.

If you read Hebrews 11, you will notice that the heroes of the

Bible were rarely social climbers. They were people who gave their lives to God and trusted that He would lead His children to develop their fullest potential, without hurting others. This is difficult to put into practice, especially if you are in a competitive line of work. In such occupations you do need drive, ambition, and persistence. But recognize too, that God has given each of us gifts, strengths, and abilities that should be used to serve and honor Him. How you do this, without getting caught into the worldly drive for success, may be one of the most persistent issues that you will face as you build and live out your career.

Making Changes

Steve Louden recently lost his job.

"I had been laid off before," he wrote in an insightful magazine article,

> but this time my response was much worse—perhaps because I now had responsibility for a family. As I packed my books and cleaned out my office . . . I left behind a few things—my self-esteem and my security. I became overly defensive, taking things people said as put-downs, and reacting with paranoia toward friends. I was embarrassed to tell others I was unemployed because I thought they would have a lower opinion of me. Sometimes I would mention my profession and then sidestep further questions so they would assume I was employed.
>
> I had experienced depression before and thought I would never let myself get in that situation again—but was I ever wrong![11]

Only in fairy tales do people make decisions and "live happily ever after." Finding an occupation and building a career can be stimulating activities, but there is no guarantee that our work will continue indefinitely and without interruption. Some very promising careers are halted abruptly by illness or accidents. Thousands of people with good educations and high motivation have had their career hopes dashed by an inability to find work that matches their capabilities. Economists call these the "underemployed." Others discover that unreasonable employers or hard-nosed professors can squelch professional progress, and even dedicated workers may be affected by economic trends or by a government's decision to require military service.

Each of these hindrances can create the insecurity, loss of self-esteem, and depression that Steve Louden experienced. Each of these obstacles can bring financial pressure and sometimes a radical change in roles if the wife goes to work and the unemployed husband stays home to care for the family. If your former job was fulfilling, or if your career choice was exciting, you may find yourself grieving over a lost career.

I have a friend who wanted to be a physician. He took a pre-medical course in college and told everyone that he planned to be a doctor. But he wasn't accepted into medical school, and shortly after shifting to seminary, he discovered that cancer might snuff out his plans to enter the ministry. As his wife went to work, he went into treatment, and saw hospitals not from the doctor's viewpoint but from the perspective of a patient. When his health permitted, he continued to study.

In time, my friend graduated and he also recovered. To his surprise, he was asked to become a hospital chaplain. I can't think of a person who is more qualified. His lifelong interest in the sick, his experiential understanding of the seriously ill, his spiritual commitment, and his seminary training have all suited him for the career that he never expected but now finds so fulfilling.

Not all career obstacles lead to such a happy ending. When he wrote his article, Steve Louden had sent out three hundred résumés, but he still was unemployed after two and a half years. Determining to spend some time each day in prayer and Bible reading, teaching himself to praise God even in the midst of difficult circumstances, and accepting the gentle love and concern of friends who stuck with him (even when he was "oversensitive, defensive, and sometimes downright rude") all helped this man to reexamine his values and adjust to the unsought changes in his career.

Unemployment forces us to look carefully at our dreams and vocational goals. Even if you are in a secure position, however, there is value in periodically taking what has been called a "career audit."[12] Ask yourself:

- Is this work or this job where I want to remain for the rest of my life?
- Have I already fallen into the success mentality so that I am more interested about getting ahead in my work than in serving the Lord with my life?
- Are my gifts, interests, and abilities being used where I am now working? If not, is a change feasible?
- What would I be giving up and what would I gain if I shifted jobs or changed a career at this time in life?
- What training or other education would I need to enter a new field?
- What practical steps must be taken if I change?
- Can I try out the new career without quitting my current job?
- How would my spouse respond to my making a change? What about my friends and family who know me well?
- Would my new position honor Christ?
- Am I willing to pray about my decision and seek God's leading for this possible change in careers?

If you make the change, and perhaps even if you stay with your present position, at some time you might be faced with the need to make a move geographically.[13] That can be exciting, but it also creates some new challenges as you make the transition to a new location.

Moves can be local (in the same community) or long-distance. They can be anticipated and planned, or they can be forced on us by a landlord or an employer who wants us to move. Some moves are temporary, as when a student goes to college for a few years, but other moves are permanent. Many moves are pleasant shifts to better jobs or communities, but sometimes people move "downward" because they have lost a house, a marriage, or an income. Some moves are minor relocations to some new nearby residence, while others involve the trauma of shifting many miles to a completely foreign and strange culture.

It has been suggested that moving involves four stages. First, you make the decision. If this is a job-related move, you probably hope for a better position if you relocate. If the move involves a promotion, you may be more willing to go than if you are taking the risk of moving in the hope that you might find more job opportunities in some other community.

After you make the decision, you begin the stage of getting ready and breaking ties with your old community. If you are glad to go, this separation might be easier, but if you have friends and family in the old community the prospect of leaving can bring both sadness and anxiety. Sometimes the busyness of getting ready is a protection that keeps you from facing the full impact of the coming change.

The stage of actually traveling to the new location can involve feelings of relief that everything has been packed and good-byes have been said, sadness about leaving your friends and the old familiar community, anxiety about what you might find in the new location, and excitement about the future.

Eventually, you start the stage of readjustment. Almost always there are some surprises when you move and sometimes a big gap exists between what you expected and what you found. Finding new friends, places to shop, housing, a doctor and dentist, a good church—these can all take effort and create stress. If you have a few possessions, if the family moves often, or if you enjoy moving, the adjustment may be easier. Even so, some time will pass before you feel part of a new community, and there can be tensions, especially if the husband launches into a new job and leaves his wife with the responsibilities of setting up the new household in an unfamiliar location.

Facing Vocational Realities

In seminars for young adults, more questions are raised about careers than about any other single issue. Some of these are very insightful and point to realities that young adults face during the career-launching stage of life. Could any of the following questions have been written by you?

I'm struggling with whether to enter a secular career or to go into the ministry. Which is right for me?

I'm about to graduate from college. For twenty-two years my goal has been to finish college. Now what?

Out of college for a few years, I don't have exact career goals but I feel many of my friends do. I'm torn between wanting to sort out the confusion and getting on with life or further schooling. I feel strange and a bit inferior because I don't have this all figured out already.

I'm satisfied with the way my life is going. I don't seem to have problems except for this: How do I go through life doing what I'm doing but still be satisfied? Is there something else I should be doing? Is this all there is? Should I be satisfied?

I once asked a business executive if he was satisfied with his career. "Of course not," he replied. "If I were satisfied, I wouldn't be successful."

Throughout life it can be helpful to take those career audits, rethinking your priorities (see table 7-1) and asking God to keep you alert to His leading. In Psalms 37:34 David encouraged his readers, "Don't be impatient for the Lord to act! Keep traveling steadily along his pathway and in due season he will honor you with every blessing . . . " (TLB).

Instead of worrying or trying to jump impulsively from career to career, it is better to keep "traveling steadily" in your present job while you ponder your future directions. Ask God to give wisdom before you make any moves, and discuss your career periodically with someone who knows you well. If you, as a Christian, are diligent, available, and willing to be used by God, in His place of service, then you can know that He will work in and through your life, giving the degree of success and exposure that He wants you to have.

As you ponder this, you might also consider the problems of advancement in a career. You may share some of the concerns of the person who asked:

How do I deal with the business world, building my career, and at the same time keep my Christian values? Politics, fear, and competition are all present at work. Doing my job well apparently isn't enough. I have to learn to play games if I am to survive.

It never is easy to make ethical decisions, especially when you are dealing with areas that the Bible never mentions. The opinions of friends can help, and so can their prayers. It also can be valuable to ponder what Jesus might have done in your present situation. Of course He lived in a different culture and period of history. The people in Nazareth never faced the pressures of today's business or professional world, but one thing we do know: Jesus, the One who is our example, would have decided what is right, then He would have done it.

Could that response apply to the next question?

Much has been said about career advancement in corporations, but what about fields such as nursing, skill work, the pastorate, being a homemaker? There is less "climb the ladder" atmosphere in these jobs, but how do such people, including me, measure their progress and growth?

It isn't easy to measure success, especially when there are no bosses to tell us how we are doing. When I write a book, I sit alone in this little office and wonder if my work is poor, acceptable, or good. In a few years, after the book has been out for a while, I might see some reviews, but that doesn't help now, at the time when I work to write the words.

To keep growing, I ask God daily to give me the desire and the ability to do a good job. I don't spend much time comparing my work with that of others, but I do try to improve on my own past performance. My goal is to make this manuscript better than the last. By competing with myself, I don't hurt anybody and I am motivated to keep improving.

All of this talk about career management is fine but it overlooks my problem which is one of relaxation. How do I balance my work with my need for leisure? I tend to be a workaholic, who is too busy to rest and not attentive enough to my wife and young daughter.

It is easy to let our lives get out of balance, to get caught up in work, and to forget our families and the need for relaxation. The problem is especially acute if you work for a company that expects your total commitment, if you are in a job where there literally is no time for leisure, or if you are in a ministry or other profession where you believe in the importance of "giving your all" for the work.

Most busy people know that they should slow down. The problem comes in turning this knowledge into action. Too often we become what one psychologist[14] has called "leisure avoiders," who give lip service to the idea of slowing down but do nothing about it; we become "leisure blenders," who take time to relax but who always seem to mix this with work, squeezing a mini-vacation into a business trip, for example, or looking for business contacts even when on vacation; or we are "leisure ruminators," who actually take time off but who never forget the work we left behind. Maybe you don't fit into any of these three categories, but it is sobering to realize how easily people develop these ways of thinking as they get more involved in their careers.

How do you separate work from leisure and keep from slipping into the workaholic mentality?

Start by pondering the real value of relaxation. Leisure isn't simply fun. It is a necessary part of life. We need time for leisure if we hope to build family relationships, manage stress, avoid burnout, and increase the overall productivity and quality of our work. Even Jesus took time to relax from His busy schedule. God created the world in six days and rested on the seventh. Who are we to think that all work and no play is healthy? Perhaps leisure is especially needed when the work load is heavy and you feel under pressure.

Once you are convinced that rejuvenation is important, set aside regular periods to relax. Don't try to schedule large blocks of time, at least when you begin. If the leisure time period is too big, you will be tempted to abandon your plan quickly. Instead, begin with smaller amounts of time and try to increase this later.

Then, recognize that relaxation is not meant to be a goal-directed activity. Some people decide to relax by getting involved with sports, but when they start competing with themselves or others, the "relaxation" has become another source of pressure. The people who have most trouble relaxing are often those who like competition, evaluations of performance, planning for the future, and making things happen. If these attitudes are allowed to intrude on your leisure times, you have undercut what relaxation is supposed to accomplish. Try, then, to experience things—like a sunset, a sauna, a swim—without analyzing them.

As you move in this direction, expect and confront uncomfortable feelings. It is common to feel guilty, self-condemning, or anxious. Ask God to help you resist these attitudes. Remember that leisure time serves a useful purpose and is consistent with Christian commitment.

Learning to relax, choosing a vocation, building a career, handling the changes that our jobs demand, and facing the realities of our work, can all be challenging, fulfilling, and frustrating. God gave us the responsibility to work diligently, but He also showed us that work must not dominate our lives—even when we are young and just getting started.

As you ponder your career, you might remember these words of John Wanamaker: "People who cannot find time for recreation are obliged sooner or later to find time for illness" and, we might add, ultimate failure.

Table 7-1
Setting Life Goals

It is easy to drift through life, moving from one job to another, without much real purpose or direction. In contrast, people whose lives are most fulfilling and productive often are those who have set some goals and established priorities for their careers, families, and personal-spiritual development.

Setting goals and priorities is not a once-in-a-lifetime experience. With some frequency, throughout life, it is helpful to reevaluate where you are going. The following guidelines may be useful.

1. Begin with prayer. Ask God to help you set goals and priorities that honor Him and make best use of your God-given gifts and abilities.

2. In two or three sentences, write your purpose in life. This will not be easy, and you may want to revise your sentences later. Having some general purposes (e.g., to be a good parent, to honor God in my work, to be as good as possible in my profession) can give your life a direction. In Colossians 1:28, 29, Paul states his life purpose.

3. Write down some specific life goals. Good goals are:
   —specific and definite in terms of what you expect;
   —achievable in a certain time span;
   —realistic, practical, and feasible;
   —limited to one goal in each statement;
   —measurable, in that you will be able to tell whether or not the goal has been reached;
   —both short-term (what you hope to accomplish within the next few weeks) and long-range (your goals for this year, the next five years, or the next decade).

4. Ask these questions about each of your goals:
   —Can the goal be accomplished?
   —Does the goal have a date when I aim to have it attained?

—Is the goal so specific that I will be able to know when I have achieved it?

—Do I have, or can I get the financial resources and training to attain the goal?[15]

5. For each goal, set up a series of steps for reaching the goal. Each step should be simple (not too complicated or too difficult), practical, specific, and in logical sequence. When this is completed you should know for each goal, "What do I do first?"

6. Put your goals in order of priority. Write an *A* beside the "must do" goals; a *B* beside the "should do" goals; and a *C* beside the "nice to do" goals.

7. Decide which goal or goals to work on first. When will you start?

8. Think about your motivation. At the beginning your enthusiasm might keep you going, but in time you probably will get tired or discouraged. To keep yourself going, you might motivate yourself with charts (like the daily calorie intake chart that the dieter might post on the refrigerator door). As you complete each step, you could reward yourself with some activity, recreation, or purchase, but don't reward yourself until you accomplish the goal. Think of some other person to whom you could give reports about your progress or lack of progress toward your goals.

9. Remind yourself of these words from Proverbs 16:3 and 9: "Commit to the Lord whatever you do, and your plans will succeed. . . . In his heart a man plans his course, but the Lord determines his steps."

Table 7-2
Getting Control of Time

Time is one of the few things in this life that each of us has in an equal amount. But nothing more clearly divides people than the ways in which we handle our time.

It is easy to complain about not having enough time, about having time on our hands, or about wasting time. Often we remark that time is passing quickly or that others steal our time. By applying several principles, however, we discover that instead of losing time, we can learn to control and manage it effectively.[16]

1. Admit to yourself that you will never get complete control of your time; neither will you be able to stop all interruptions and distractions (and that is probably okay).

2. Recognize, however, that it is possible to get better control of your time, providing you are determined to do so.

3. Realize that while others steal your time, you may be the biggest time waster of all. It is you who makes the difference in time management.

4. For one week, keep a record of how you spend your time. This task will take effort—and time—but it also will let you see what is happening to your minutes and hours. Such awareness is a basic step for getting control of your time.

5. Try to determine what is stealing your time: Are you wasting time because you lack clear daily and weekly goals? Do you get distracted with time-consuming activities that could wait until later? Are you trying to do more than time allows, and constantly experiencing frustrations because you can't get things done? Do you let yourself get distracted by television, unopened mail, daydreaming, or other time wasters?

6. End each day by planning the next day. List what needs to be done and make an estimate of the time needed for each

activity. Rank the listed items in order of importance. Plan some time for unexpected interruptions. Roughly determine when (during the day) you will tackle each item.

7. Enlist the help of others. Ask them to keep from interrupting you and to respect your need, at times, to pull away and to get things done.

8. Use gimmicks, if necessary. Make a chart of your time use, for example, and keep a record of your efficiency. Reward yourself with a break or a brief distraction whenever you work for a solid block of time without interrupting yourself.

9. Group activities. Try to handle all the mail or phone calls at once, for example. If you are involved in one project and think of another, make a note of the second project and schedule time to do it later.

10. Challenge your own thinking. Is it really true that others are taking your time, that you can't find the needed time, or that you will do some project "later when I have time"? Remember, you are in control of much of your time.

11. Look at your interruptions. Are you letting them happen? Are you giving others the message that it is okay to interrupt you at any time?

12. Plan ahead realistically. You can get worried and inefficient if you are constantly overwhelmed by all that needs to be done. Plan ahead and things will get done.

13. Divide and conquer. Divide big projects into smaller tasks that can be managed. Books are written one word at a time. Your time-consuming projects can be divided into "doable" segments.

14. Recognize that God expects you to make good use of your time. According to the Bible, you should "make the best use of your time, despite all the evils of these days" (Ephesians 5:16 PHILLIPS).

15. Don't become so concerned about time management that you become compulsive and unable to relax. "Slow me down, Lord," an unknown writer once wrote. "Steady my

hurried pace with a vision of the eternal reach of time.... Teach me the art of taking minute vacations—of slowing down to look at a flower, to chat with a friend, to pat a dog, to read a few lines from a good book."

Source Notes

1. M. Scott Peck, *The Road Less Traveled* (New York: Simon and Schuster [A Touchstone Book], 1978), p. 15.

2. Ibid., p. 17.

3. There are guides published to help people plan careers. These include Richard Bolles, *What Color Is Your Parachute?* rev. ed. (Berkeley, Calif.: Ten Speed Press, 1978); Kirk E. Farnsworth and Wendell H. Lawhead, *Life Planning: A Christian Approach to Careers* (Downers Grove, Ill.: Inter-Varsity, 1981); and Richard E. Rusbuldt, *Planning Your Life* (Valley Forge, Pa.: Judson, 1978).

4. Edith Schaeffer, *The Tapestry* (Waco, Tex.: Word, 1981), pp. 421, 432, 433, 438.

5. Ibid., pp. 431, 433.

6. H. L. Wilensky, "Orderly Careers and Social Participation: The Impact of Work History on Social Integration in the Middle Mass," *American Sociological Review,* vol. 26, 1961, pp. 521–539.

7. R. P. Quinn and G. L. Staines, *The 1977 Quality of Employment Survey* (Ann Arbor, Mich.: Institute for Social Research, 1979).

8. Daniel J. Levinson et al., *The Seasons of a Man's Life* (New York: Alfred A. Knopf, 1978), pp. 97–101.

9. Joan L. Guest, "We Are Driven: The Success Syndrome and How It Affects You," *His,* vol. 49, October 1979, p. 1.

10. Trina Paulus, *Hope for the Flowers* (New York: Paulist Press, 1972).

11. Steve Louden, "Down and Out of a Job," *Discipleship Journal,* vol. 3, January 1983, p. 44.

12. Bridgford Hunt, "Career Audits Yield Surprising Results," *Pace,* vol. 9, September/October 1982, pp. 77, 94.

13. Some of these paragraphs are adapted from chapter 7, "Geographic Moves and Migrations," in Naomi Golan, *Passing Through Transitions* (New York: The Free Press, 1981).

14. Bruce A. Baldwin, "Decontaminating Your Leisure: Cornerstone of Lifestyle Management," *Pace,* vol. 9, September/October 1982, pp. 11, 14–17. The next several paragraphs are adapted from the Baldwin article.

15. These questions are suggested by Ted Engstrom, "Goals That Mobilize," *Pastoral Renewal,* vol. 5, October 1980, pp. 1–3. Several books are available, dealing with goal setting and work management. See, for example, John W. Alexander, *Managing Our Work* (Downers Grove, Ill.: Inter-Varsity, 1972); or Ted W. Engstrom and David J. Juroe, *The Work Trap* (Old Tappan, N.J.: Fleming H. Revell, 1979).

16. For a helpful treatment of time management, see Robert D. Rutherford, *Just in Time: Immediate Help for the Time-Pressured* (New York: Wiley, 1981).

8

Becoming Spiritually Mature

Handling Your Relationship With God

Recently, I celebrated an anniversary. It was a quiet celebration. There were no banners, gifts, cards, parades, or fireworks. It wasn't mentioned in the newspaper or on the TV news. My wife didn't even know about it until I remembered to mention it to her, in passing. But for me it was an interesting event to ponder. Twenty years earlier the president of Purdue University had signed a diploma that gave me a doctorate in psychology.

It had taken a lot of work for me to reach that milestone. I was never a strong student. It was a combination of youthful determination, dogged persistence, and the patience of a small army of teachers that moved me from kindergarten to graduate school and on to the the day when I finally earned the right to call myself a psychologist.

In the last two decades, I have read many criticisms of my profession. Some seem to be biased and inaccurate, but others have been well researched and thought-provoking. Around the time of my anniversary, for example, a clinical psychologist named Bernie Zilbergeld published an insightful critique of counseling and argued that therapy is neither as needed nor as effective as we might like to believe.[1]

According to Dr. Zilbergeld, many people in America accept some assumptions about life that aren't necessarily true. We conclude, for example, that the world is best understood in psychological terms, that people are not okay as they are, that everyone needs and can benefit from therapy, that we have a right to happiness, that all problems can be solved, and that psychology is the best route to personal fulfillment. Perhaps it isn't surprising that America has been called the "world capital of psychological-mindedness and therapeutic endeavor."[2] A famous member of the profession once predicted that the day could come when "there will be more psychologists than people in this country."[3]

I mention all of this because it seems that some of my fellow Christians have followed our society into thinking that the hope for our generation is found in psychology. Zilbergeld titled his book *The Shrinking of America* but I wonder if there hasn't also been a "shrinking of the church." Pastoral counseling, marriage enrichment, possibility thinking, personal enhancement, transparency development, self-help groups, stress- and time-management seminars, psychologically based fund-raising and advertising campaigns—these and a number of other psychological influences have slipped into the local congregation. Such trends are not necessarily bad. Since becoming a psychologist, I have encouraged many of them myself. But even good and useful psychological ideas can distract from a basic Christian assumption: Our hope is in the Lord.[4]

When Simon Peter wrote his second epistle, influences more dangerous than psychology were seeping into the church and distracting the early believers from sound doctrine. After reminding the readers of God's righteousness, grace, peace, and power, the epistle writer made the remarkable statement that God has given us everything we need to live a good life.[5] Christian living is not meant to be what someone has called "an initial spasm followed by a chronic inertia."[6] Instead, we are to accept what God has promised and then make diligent and consistent effort to live lives that are characterized by faith, goodness, knowledge, self-control, perseverance, godliness, kindness, and love.[7]

Such thinking is foreign both to contemporary psychology and to the daily lives of most young (and older) adults in our society. The people with whom Christians work, study, relax, do business, and live, often have values that are far removed from the teachings of the Bible. This presents most of us with some strong dilemmas. How can we live in ways that are vocationally successful and pleasing to Christ when we are part of a society that rejects Christian principles?

Several young adults have expressed their concerns about these issues in seminars I have taught:

As a Christian, how do I relate to my non-Christian friends and family members? What are my responsibilities?

As life gets busier for me, how can I find time to read the Bible and pray?

Often I am unsure about my beliefs. My Christian walk is always going up and down. Is this normal?

How do I overcome the "keeping up with the Joneses" philosophy? I'm always worrying about impressing others with material things to show how successful I have been. What does God say about this? How can I quit comparing myself with others?

It isn't easy for me to turn my burdens over to the Lord and then to leave them with Him. Instead, I worry a lot. How can I handle this spiritual struggle?

How does one keep his eyes on Christ and still have the drive and time to succeed in business? How can I be a good Christian example in the business world?

How do I fit in the church when they think I am too young and inexperienced to do anything?

It's hard for me to be patient and to trust God to bring my dreams and aspirations together.

How do I bring Christ into my profession without pushing my beliefs onto others? My profession considers that unethical.

In this chapter we will look at some of these issues as they relate to the Christian's professional life. We will consider how faith in Christ can influence our personal and prayer lives. The place to start, however, is with a look at our private lives.

The Christian's Private Life

Long before Christ was born, God spoke to a man named Abraham and told him to move. There were no moving companies to help the man's family relocate, and at that point they didn't even know where they would be going. Nevertheless, without hesitation, Abraham obeyed.

This was the story of his life. Consistently he trusted the Lord and followed His commands even when the instructions seemed strange and illogical. When God told the old man to sacrifice his only son, for example, Abraham decided immediately to obey. The young boy was placed on the altar until God stopped the proceedings and provided a sacrificial lamb instead. In accordance with the custom of that time and country, Abraham gave a name to the place where this happened. He called it *Jehovah-jireh*. The words mean "The Lord will provide."[8]

I've often thought about this in my own life. God has promised to provide all that we need,[9] but do I really believe He will do this? I have no doubt that He *can* provide; but sometimes, when there are important decisions to be made or when our family has special financial needs, doubt raises its ugly head and I wonder if He *will* provide as He has promised.

I suspect my thinking is not unique. It is difficult to believe that God will provide the resources, wisdom, patience, and opportunities we need to get through this life. We are part of a culture that praises individual drive, planning, initiative, and creativity. We are not used to seeking divine guidance before we forge ahead with our plans. Even Christians admire the "self-made man or woman," and we aren't inclined to give much thought to the fact that everything we have and do depends on God.

Philip Yancey is one of my favorite writers, not only because of his way with words but also because of his penetrating insights. "Self-sufficiency is the most fatal sin because it pulls us, as if by a magnet, from God," he wrote in a recent book.

> Tensions and anxieties flame within me the moment I forget I am living my life for the one-man audience of Christ and slip into living my life to assert myself in a competitive world.
>
> Previously, my main motivation in life was to do a painting of myself, filled with bright colors and profound insights, so that all who looked upon it would be impressed. Now, however, I find that my role is to be a mirror, to brightly reflect the image of God through me. Or perhaps the metaphor of stained glass would serve better, for, after all, God will illuminate through my personality and body....
>
> I no longer find my identity in my apartness from the rest of the world. Now, I find it in my sameness. I am exactly the same as everyone in the world in terms of my standing before God—I am a sinner....
>
> I cannot imagine a more difficult stumbling block in Christianity. It is relatively easy to inspire people with the Christian ethic of love.... But every mechanism of self-protection within me cries out against this painful, renouncing step of identifying myself as a sinner.[10]

If there could be no hope beyond this realization, our lives would be futile and in true existential despair. But God, in His wisdom, sent Jesus Christ to pay for our sins. We are not forced to accept or to believe that this really happened; humans, at their peril, are free to reject Christ. But if we confess our sin and acknowledge that Jesus is Lord, He forgives, and completely changes our lives.[11]

Yancey has commented on the effects of this decision:

> After going through the humiliating act of losing myself by letting go of that protective pride, I suddenly find myself with a new identity—the exalted state that Paul describes as "in-Christness." No longer must I defend my thoughts, my values, my actions. I trade those in for the identity I am given as a son of God. . . .
>
> My sense of competition quickly fades. No longer do I have to bristle through life, racking up points to prove myself. My role has ideally become to prove God, to live in such a way that people around me recognize Jesus and his love, not the other set of qualities which separate me from the world. I have found this process to be healthy, relaxing, and wholly good.[12]

The writer of those words has a life that is different, not only because he has made a complete commitment to Christ, but also because there has been a change in his private thinking.

Have you ever heard it said that "as a man thinks, so he is"? If we could really know how another person thinks, we would have an accurate picture of what that person is like.

Thinking is part of our private lives. The only ones who really know what or how I think are God, me, and anyone to whom I choose to reveal my thoughts. Nevertheless, if my thinking tends to be critical, competitive, or complacent, that will mold my actions, color my emotions, and shape my personality. If, in contrast, I have a positive, grateful outlook on life, or if I believe, like Abraham, that the Lord will always provide, these ideas also influence me significantly.

The committed and maturing Christian seeks to think in ways that would please Christ.[13] Of course our minds wander and our perspectives get distorted, but life is healthier and less pressured if our private thinking is consistent with biblical teaching. How powerful are the inspired words of the New Testament writer who wrote: "whatever is true, whatever is honorable, whatever is right, whatever is pure, whatever is lovely, whatever is of good repute, if there is any excellence and if anything worthy of praise, let your mind dwell on these things."[14] Such thinking has a positive influence on us psychologically, and it spills over to influence the ways in which we live our personal lives.

The Christian's Personal Life

A twenty-four-year-old woman recently called a Christian radio station to participate in a talk show. She reported that she was a believer, divorced from her first husband, and living with a man to whom she was not married. She admitted that her life-style was not consistent with biblical teachings and expressed some concern that her male friend was not a believer.

"Have you talked with him about Christ or told him about your beliefs?" the program host asked.

"No," the caller responded. "I believe religious belief is a private matter. It's just between God and me. It is too personal to talk about with someone else."

At the midpoint of this century, a respected Harvard psychologist wrote that sex and religion seem to have reversed their positions.[15] In earlier decades we talked openly about our beliefs, but reserved sexual comments and behavior for the bedroom. Now sex is discussed freely, but we are embarrassed to say much about our beliefs or to let them influence our daily actions.

Such an attitude would have been unthinkable in the early church. The first Christians made more than an intellectual commitment to Christ. They determined to let Him mold their thinking, their marriages, their work, their values, and their futures. In short, Christ influenced their whole lives.

Are Christians any different today? Does Christ make a practical difference in your personal life, or in mine? To answer these questions, we must give some thought to the issue of life-styles.

Suppose somebody could follow you around for a few weeks and see how you related to other people, spent your time or money, and reacted to events in your environment. Before long, your follower would notice that you tend to react to situations in similar ways. These similarities are what we mean by life-style. According to the man who first used the word, a *life-style* is "a person's unique and characteristic pattern of relating to his world and environment."[16]

After observing counselees for several years, psychologist Emery Nester concluded that a healthy life-style has five features.[17]

First, there must be firm personal commitments. If you are committed to a person or to a cause, you do not allow danger, discouragement, or inconvenience to distract you. Your thinking and your actions are directed toward the object of commitment, and you keep that object clearly in mind.

Among other things, I am committed to my marriage, to my children, to accuracy in my writing, and to honesty in my dealings with other people. Such commitments make a practical difference in how I live. In contrast, I'm not committed to politics or to a push to become well-known. Because I don't care a lot about these things, they rarely influence my behavior or affect the way I think.

If we are really committed to following Jesus Christ, that will make a practical difference in our life-styles. The example of Abraham is relevant once again.

Dr. Nester believes that depression is especially common among young adults. He describes people under thirty as "the generation of depressives," and goes on to suggest that *one* of the reasons for depression is that people don't have any commitments.[18] What about you?

A second feature of the healthy life-style is for one to have an adequate philosophy of life. You might want to ask yourself three questions. In your opinion, what is real? What is true? What is good? It could be helpful to write down your answers.

This is a difficult assignment, but what you write is a good indication of your philosophy of life. That philosophy influences how you live.

A willingness to admit that we are human is a third feature of the healthy life-style. Perhaps there is a perfectionistic streak in all of us. We don't like to admit that we are weak or that we "goof." Many men don't like to admit that they hurt or cry. Christians are reluctant to acknowledge that they lust or are greedy.

It is natural to be disappointed, to feel angry, to cry or laugh, to make mistakes or to think negative thoughts. We might not like some of these human characteristics, and we might have difficulty changing, especially for the better, but to admit our humanness is to move toward greater spiritual and psychological health. To admit our humanness also brings a more relaxed and less hectic life-style.

Fourth, the healthy life-style is characterized by an inner sense of direction. When a person has clear goals in life it is easy to feel a sense of direction, but what if you don't yet have clear goals? Must you flounder?

Not if you are a Christian. According to the Bible, God's Holy Spirit lives within the believer and guides our lives so that our behavior is more Christlike.[19] None of us needs to be swayed by circumstances or pushed about by the actions of others. We are not like mules who need to be led in a mindless way. "I will instruct you," said the Lord. "I will counsel you and watch over you."[20] Such inner guidance gives us a sense of direction.

Finally, people with healthy life-styles are able to accept the fact that they are unique. Sometimes we resent our idiosyncrasies and complain because we are not like others whom we admire. But we can be glad that, like snowflakes, every one of us has been made as a unique creation of God. We have special gifts, abilities, and personalities. All of these help to mold our life-styles. All have a bearing on our vocational or professional lives.

The Christian's Professional Life

I know a nurse who used to work in the office of a local private practitioner. The doctor is a Christian, an active church member, and a man who, in his medical work, adamantly refuses to mention Christ or to let his beliefs be known to the patients. The doctor's employees have been told that it is unethical to mention religion in the office or hospital room. Frustrated over this muzzling policy, my nurse friend recently quit her job.

Most professional people would agree, I suspect, that it is not appropriate to be preaching when we should be providing medical, psychological, dental, or other professional services. I once read of a physician who covered his waiting room with wallpaper printed with Bible verses. He was criticized, even by his fellow believers, and rightly so. But for Christians, isn't it also unethical, if not blatantly sinful, to pretend that Christ has no relevance to the needs of patients? When people are facing crises and even death, isn't is wrong to erect a rigid barrier between our professional mannerisms and our knowledge of the gospel message?

The question goes far beyond medical practice. Can we really hope to mature spiritually or claim to be serving Christ obediently if we divorce our beliefs from our businesses? If we believe that Christ is to be Lord of our lives, He must be Lord of our vocations. How, then, can we serve Him effectively at work without alienating our employers and fellow workers or without taking advantage of our clients and employees?

The Book of Colossians gives a partial answer: "Whatever you do, work at it with all your heart, as working for the Lord, not for men. . . . It is the Lord Christ you are serving."[21] Here, again, is an emphasis on attitudes and ways of thinking. As we work, we must keep in mind that in everything we are serving the Lord. That means that we will strive to be honest, industrious, and effective in our work. We might not have opportunity to say much about our faith, but in time people will know we are different because of our diligence and dedication to competence. Here is a practical example of letting our "light" shine before others so they can see our "good works" and honor the Father who is in heaven.[22]

In the little New Testament Book of Titus, we read about the qualifications of church leaders.[23] Presumably these standards were intended to be high. Not everyone could pass the test. These requirements are specific, however, and they give goals that could guide all of us in our vocations.

In life and work, let us strive to be

- blameless: people whose actions are above reproach;
- sensitive to our family needs;
- not troublemakers, overbearing, insensitive, self-willed, quick-tempered, violent, greedy people;
- individuals who are hospitable, loving what is good, self-

controlled, fair, devout, disciplined and "not addicted" to
alcohol;

* committed to biblical teaching; and
* inclined to encourage others, to state what we believe, and
  to refute the theological error.

If we believe that the Holy Spirit guides our lives, we can
expect that He will help us develop these traits and give us
guidance in terms of when to express our faith verbally and
when to keep quiet but give a silent witness.

As Christians, we respect those people who disagree with our
beliefs. It *is* unethical to force theology on our fellow workers
and business or professional associates, but the Great Com-
mission forbids us to keep silent forever. I disagree with the
talk-show caller who thinks religion is so personal that we
don't even mention it to our roommates. In our era of change
and uncertainty, many people are searching for an anchor of
stability and hope. Even in a nation that claims to be Christian,
many have never heard the gospel. We have a responsibility to
share the Good News, but not in a stilted, stereotyped, or insensitive way. Ask God to prepare minds—yours and others.
Then we can trust him to guide our conversations so that "wit-
nessing" becomes as natural as talking about our interests or
neighborhood activities.

Recently I had lunch with an air force chaplain who described some of the challenges of sharing and keeping one's
faith alive in a military setting. He talked of competition, of the
need to be noticed by one's superiors, of the importance of
hiding problems or insecurities lest these become known and
used as evidence to block a promotion. What my friend sees in
the military, permeates civilian life as well. It is professional
suicide to be honest or humble. People who don't show drive
and competition don't get promotions. In many places, ap-

parently including doctors' offices and military bases, it can be a vocational disadvantage to even mention one's beliefs.

There is no easy way out of these dilemmas. There are no set rules concerning how we bring our faith into our vocations. We can only be willing to have God use us. In time He will—sometimes even without our awareness.

What we do need is an awareness of who God is and what He wants for His children. We can't bring God into our professional lives unless He is an integrated part of our personal lives. This brings us to the issue of prayer.

The Christian's Prayer Life

Tucked in the shelves of my bookcase are perhaps a dozen books describing "contemporary" college students. I've collected these volumes over the years and have noticed how the descriptions of students have changed. There was a time when religion was not a popular subject on campus. Later there arose a student generation that had great interest in the Jesus movement and another was fascinated with the idea of being "born again." More recently, cults have captured student minds, and universities have seen an explosion of interest in religion courses. The latest addition to my bookshelves says that religious commitment among students is dropping, that college-age adults are tired of the traditional church, but that parachurch organizations are alive and active. The same report finds that students are pessimistic about the country but optimistic about their personal futures. In preparing for the years ahead, they are like people "going first class on the Titanic."[24]

Do you see any of these attitudes in yourself or in your friends? Are there young adults who sail through life, caught up in its pleasures and successes, but with little awareness of the dangers or obstacles that might lurk ahead? In building lives, careers, and marriages, have we forgotten the Creator, who is available like a pilot, to help us navigate through life? Has religion for many people become little more than a three-credit college course?

Not long ago, I reached a new stage in parenthood. My eldest daughter, who had just turned sixteen and finally was in possession of a driver's license, drove off by herself to a meeting in another town. I had watched her drive many times before. She had shown that she was a good driver, and I knew she would be careful. But she was also inexperienced, and less aware of the dangers than her slightly nervous father, who watched as the car backed out of the driveway.

After she left that morning, I wondered if God looks at His children in similar ways. We have only limited experience with life and spiritual things. As we move on this journey through life, we could make costly and dangerous errors in judgment. In a country where interest in God and spiritual things keeps changing, we could move far away from the One who created us. We could build values and develop life-styles that give immediate pleasure but ultimately are self-defeating.

How do we avoid this? In an earlier chapter we talked about skills: stress-managment skills, communication skills, child-rearing skills, life-planning skills, and time-management skills—to mention a few. Is it possible that we can also develop spiritual-growth skills? Just as consistent practicing is needed to improve the pianist's musical skills and abilities, so consistent time with the Lord—"practicing the presence of God," to use Brother Lawrence's term—is a prerequisite for spiritual growth.

Over the centuries, thousands of books have been written to give instructions on spiritual skills and growth. Go to any library or Christian bookstore and you will find books on prayer, Bible study, and personal religious devotions. Some of these are very helpful, although they are far too detailed to be summarized here.[25] Instead, let us look briefly at the spiritual actions of Jesus. How did He relate to His heavenly Father?

First, Jesus prayed. Prayer was at the center of His life. He prayed in the temple. He prayed alone. He prayed as He went about His daily activities. He prayed before meals, before making decisions, before doing God's work, and before facing crises. He who was the Son of God knew that prayer was crucial. Can it be any less important for His followers? If we want spiritual power and growth, we have no alternative but to take time to communicate with God in prayer.

Prayer is the offering to God of our praise and desires. It involves adoration, honest confession, the giving of thanks, the expressing of our commitment to Him, and the sharing of our petitions. Prayer, it has been suggested, "should concern itself less and less with the sort of petition that says 'give me, give me.' Such prayers will recede as they are replaced by earnest petition that God will grant wisdom and strength with which the servant may meet his needs and measure up to the high calling of God."[26]

Second, in addition to the importance of prayer, it is clear that the spirituality of Jesus was related to His knowledge of the Scriptures. How easy it is to hear sermons and read *about* God, while we fail to spend time listening directly *to* God. He speaks to us in a variety of ways, including through books and sermons, but nothing is clearer than the message that comes directly through a consistent study of the Bible.

Bible study can be done in different ways: by reading and meditating, by taking notes, by small group discussion with other Christians, by using Bible study guides, by memorizing verses. Like me, you may have used them all, and more. Probably you realize that a method may work well for one person and not for another. We each have times and places for Bible reading which suit us best.

Each of us may also find that it is easy to get distracted and to put off spending time with God. Somehow other pressing activities always seem to be more important than times of meditation. Even dedicated Christians find that it is easy to push God into the background and to hurry through our days giving lip service, but little time or thought to the Lord. Rarely do we face the fact that spiritual growth only comes to those who are disciplined enough to spend time with God—time alone and time spent at worship in the company of other believers.

Back in graduate school, before they gave me that psychology degree, I decided to spend at least a brief time alone with God each day, and to be consistent in Sunday worship. Little interfered with this decision, although I was, and am, constantly tempted to push God aside because of other demands. In our own strength it is difficult, perhaps impossible, to walk consistently with God. But the Holy Spirit helps us, not only to pray and to meditate, but to understand and apply the truths of Scripture.

A group of people once came to engage Jesus in a theological debate. Far from having a casual interest in religion, these people were the professional theologians of their day. They were spiritual leaders, but Jesus recognized that they were also spiritually ignorant and spiritually dead. He stated the reason for this in one powerful sentence.

"You are in error because you do not know the scriptures or the power of God."[27]

What an indictment. Could the same be said of you or of me? The way to know the Scriptures and the power of God is to spend time in prayer and in reading God's Word.

Jesus knew this, but He was not a recluse who lived a contemplative life far removed from the daily pressures and politics of His society. Jesus prayed. Jesus knew the Scriptures. And Jesus reached out to others.

Serving, caring, encouraging, sharing, helping—these are all part of the Christian message. There is no such thing as a self-centered Christianity. Contemplation and compassion, personal prayer and practical people-helping, quiet meditation and active outreach—these are like two sides of a coin. There can't be real Christian growth without both personal spiritual discipline and public willing service.

For many people, it seems that religion is largely irrelevant to the modern world. There is little time for God, little recognition that He is needed, little interest in His teaching, and almost no inclination to obey His commandments. The founder of a big hamburger franchise expressed the modern viewpoint concisely. "I speak of faith in McDonald's as if it were a religion," he is reported to have said. "I believe in God, family and McDonald's—and in the office that order is reversed."[28] Such a viewpoint isn't good Christianity. Ultimately, this isn't good business either.

Looking back over my two decades as a psychologist, I have been impressed with two conclusions. First, modern psychology can help us to live more effectively, to cope with problems, and to mature as individuals. Much of psychology may be a gift from God to help us with the pressures of living.

But (this is my second conclusion) psychology, like every other area of study, is limited when it fails to recognize the power of God. It is He who gives everything that we need "for life and godliness."[29] The psychology in this and other books can be helpful, but true fulfillment, personal growth, and spiritual maturity come only when we place our lives under God's control and trust Him to guide in the day-to-day activities of moving through adulthood.

Table 8-1
How to Handle Spiritual Dryness[30]

For many Christians, the spiritual life is like riding a roller coaster. There are ups and downs, high points and low, periods of anticipation and excitement, followed by quick returns to the normal routine of life. This surely is not what God intended, but it is a common experience.

At times, most of us hit periods of spiritual dryness. Sometimes for days or months we trudge through discouragement, unhappiness, restlessness, and feelings of inefficiency. We read the Bible, but it doesn't seem to say much. We go to church, but the services seem dull and meaningless. Prayer feels like an empty habit. Our consciences become dull and insensitive. There is little joy and no enthusiasm over spiritual things.

When this happens it can be helpful to honestly consider the following ten questions.

1. *Am I believer?* It is impossible to be alive spiritually if you have not been born spiritually. This is what is meant by being "born again." Talk to Jesus Christ in prayer. Ask Him to forgive your sins. Tell Him you believe He is Lord and ask Him to take control of your life.

2. *Am I sinning?* Everybody sins at times, but if we fail to confess our sins or if we keep sinning, we go down spiritually. First John 1:9 promises that if we confess our sins, Christ will forgive us and cleanse us. Most of us have to confess frequently.

3. *Am I out of shape physically?* Does it surprise you to find this on the list? When we don't take care of our bodies, we run down physically and this can affect our spiritual lives as well.

4. *Am I spiritually undernourished?* When we are too busy for periods of prayer, Bible study, and worship, we lose our spiritual vitality—just as we would lose our physical vitality if we didn't take time to eat or to rest.

5. *Am I spiritually overfed?* Just as we can be undernourished spiritually, we can also be overfed and spiritually bloated. The essence of Christianity is loving and giving. We can decline spiritually if we take in spiritual ideas but never share anything or never give prayer support, encouragement, money, time, or service to others.

6. *Am I legalistic and hypercritical?* A holier-than-thou attitude usually indicates pride. It is right to point out error, but if we speak the truth it must be in an attitude of love, and without judgment.

7. *Am I thinking clearly?* It is easy to get things out of perspective, to criticize when we don't have accurate facts, and to get caught up in the world's values of status seeking and self-centered struggles to get ahead. Another believer can help you keep your values and thinking in a clearer and more accurate perspective.

8. *Is my life unbalanced?* We can get too involved in work, in church activities, in sports, in dating, in family life, even in prayer. At such times life gets out of balance. For spiritual vitality we need a balance between work and rest, solitude and social involvement, individual and family activities, along with a willingness both to learn from others and to give creatively in return.

9. *Am I spiritually powered?* The Holy Spirit lives within the believer, but He can be ignored, squelched, or pushed aside. We need to confess our sins daily and ask the Holy Spirit to give us wisdom, guidance, stability, and power.

10. *Am I too independent?* Christians need each other. Spiritual growth is stunted when we fail to worship together with other believers (Hebrews 10:25).

Source Notes

1. Bernie Zilbergeld, *The Shrinking of America: Myths of Psychological Change* (Boston: Little, Brown, 1983).
2. Ibid., p. 33.
3. The quotation is from E. G. Boring, quoted in Zilbergeld, ibid., p. 87.
4. Psalms 71:5; 146:5.
5. 2 Peter 1:1–4.
6. This statement, attributed to Moffatt, is cited in William Barclay, *The Letters of James and Peter* (Philadelphia: Westminster, 1958), p. 354.
7. 2 Peter 1:5–9.
8. Hebrews 11:8–19. Jehovah-jireh is mentioned in Genesis 22:14.
9. Philippians 4:19.
10. Philip Yancey, *Open Windows* (Westchester, Ill.: Crossway, 1982), pp. 213, 210–11. Used by permission.
11. 1 John 1:9; 2 Corinthians 5:17.
12. Yancey, op. cit.
13. 1 Corinthians 2:16; Philippians 2:5.
14. Philippians 4:8, NASB.
15. Gordon W. Allport, *The Individual and His Religion* (New York: Macmillan, 1950), p. 1.
16. The term *life-style* and the definition of this word were first proposed many years ago by Alfred Adler.
17. Don Baker and Emery Nester, *Depression* (Portland, Ore.: Multnomah, 1983), chapter 24.
18. Baker and Nester, ibid., p. 157.
19. 1 Corinthians 6:19.
20. Psalms 32:8, 9.
21. Colossians 4:23, 24.
22. Matthew 5:16.
23. Titus 1:6–9.
24. Arthur Levine, *When Dreams and Heroes Died: A Portrait of Today's College Student* (San Francisco: Jossey-Bass, 1981), p. 98.
25. Recent books on personal spiritual development include Richard J. Foster, *Celebration of Discipline* (New York: Harper & Row, 1978); John E. Gardner, *Personal Religious Disciplines* (Grand Rapids: Wm. B. Eerdmans, 1966); Richard E. Lovelace, *Dynamics of Spiritual Life* (Downers Grove, Ill.: InterVarsity Press, 1979); John White, *The Cost of Commitment* (Downers Grove, Ill.: InterVarsity Press, 1976).
26. Gardner, ibid., p. 57.
27. Matthew 22:29.
28. Os Guinness, *The Gravedigger File* (Downers Grove, Ill.: InterVarsity Press, 1983), p. 63. The quotation is attributed to the Nov. 15, 1981, issue of *Context*, p. 6.
29. 2 Peter 1:3.

30. At the beginning of my writing career I determined to make every effort to not repeat myself and to not quote earlier works in later books. Table 8-1 is a deliberate and, I hope, rare deviation from that policy. The table comes from an article first published in *Christian Herald* magazine and later included as a chapter in Gary R. Collins, *Calm Down* (Ventura, Calif.: Vision House, 1981).

9

Becoming Established

Handling Your Settling into Adulthood

In 1831, a twenty-six-year-old Frenchman named Alexis de Tocqueville visited the United States to get a look at the new world. A member of European aristocracy, this young man apparently had time to write, and upon his return to France, he started a two-volume book that was to make him famous. Titled *Democracy in America,* de Tocqueville's work gave the perspective of someone who was both a young adult and an outside observer. Many of these observations are still being quoted because they seem so perceptive and up-to-date.

De Tocqueville concluded, for example, that we talk a lot about freedom on this side of the Atlantic, but the real striving in America is for happiness. We accept the idea that every person has a "natural right to happiness." Most of our energies are directed toward getting success, power, prestige, acquisitions, security, or anything else that might make us happy. Unlike people in other countries, we find ourselves "placed in the happiest circumstances that the world affords," but in the midst of all our prosperity and pleasures, we really are very unhappy people. One reason for this, according to de Tocqueville, is that we tend to ignore what we do have and forever are brooding over the things we don't have; things that we think could make us happy.

I wish these words applied only to previous generations, but I fear they apply to us. "It is strange to see with what feverish ardor the Americans pursue their own welfare, and to watch the vague dread that constantly torments them lest they should not have chosen the shortest path which may lead to" this well-being. Afraid that we might miss some opportunities or good experiences, many of us, says de Tocqueville, are filled with anxiety, fear, and regret. Our minds are in "ceaseless trepidation," and we are constantly moving, changing our plans, and looking for anything new that might make us happy.[1]

In contrast to this emphasis, the Bible says relatively little about happiness. When Paul was in prison, he wrote that a Christian could be content (and presumably happy) regardless of circumstances.[2] The wise apostle found happiness in his relationship with Christ.

Most of us who are Christians agree that Paul was right. Christ alone brings joy and happiness. But how difficult it is to move through adulthood without being swayed by those attitudes that de Tocqueville noticed and that we see so often in our society and in ourselves.

Moving Toward Thirty

During the early years of adulthood, many people decide to resist, reject, and try to change some of society's traditional values and attitudes. In the turbulent era of the 1960s, for example, college-age students openly rebelled against the government, against most authority, against anyone older than thirty, and against what was termed the "military-industrial complex." Traditional social values were mocked and rejected. While a shocked older generation watched in amazement, intelligent and educated young people sang songs of love and peace, but showed, sometimes violently, that they were intent on destroying the society in which they had been raised. How could anyone have known that within twenty years many of the student protesters would become established members of that society whose values they had once rejected so vehemently?

Have you ever wondered if something similar might happen to you? In the young adult years it still is possible to stand somewhat apart from the culture and to see weakness that older people no longer notice. Carried along by enthusiasm and sometimes by idealism mixed with youthful self-confidence, it is common for young people to want and expect change. When change doesn't come or when the complexities of life become obvious, it is easy to give up and stop trying to change things. Slowly, and sometimes without giving it much thought, we can drift to the conclusion that, *I can't change the establishment, so I might as well join it.*

This kind of thinking applies to one's career, but it also is reflected in attitudes toward personal growth and marriage. I know a lady who was nervous before her marriage because her parents had divorced and she had an understandable concern that the same thing could happen to her. "My parents were happy at first," she told a friend. "They were active in the church and used to tell me that they didn't believe in divorce. Then their marriage broke up. Is it possible that their values and beliefs are so ingrained in me, that I am destined to be like them? I am grateful for my mother and dad, and appreciate many of the values that they taught, but will I be inclined to repeat their mistakes?"

It *is* true that thinking is influenced both by the attitudes and the standards of our parents and culture. We are molded by our society and not able to completely shake off the early memories and social values that have been implanted within us. Deliberately as well as unconsciously, we learn by watching and imitating significant people in our lives. If your parents divorced, if your teachers were always critical, if there was tension at home, if other kids rejected you, or your father constantly stressed the importance of getting ahead in business—these things have all had a deep influence on you.

The influences do not have to be bad, however. You are different from your parents, you can learn not to repeat the mistakes of others, and you have at least some control over your own attitudes and actions. The engaged lady whose parents had divorced recognized some of the reasons for the marriage's failure. By determining not to repeat her parents' mistakes, she and her husband have been able to work at building a good marriage. I know this because I am the husband and the lady is my wife.

As they see the mistakes of others and recognize failures in their own lives, people in their twenties can become more aware of their own attitudes and of the complexities and difficulties of life. As the thirtieth birthday approaches, life appears to be more serious and we begin to realize that, "If I want to change my life and if there are things I don't like or things I want to have, now is the time to act. If I wait much longer, it might be too late."[3]

According to the researchers at Yale, these attitudes begin to surface as part of an "age thirty transition."[4] For almost a decade there has been opportunity to "find oneself" as an adult. Decisions have been made, a life-style has been formed—deliberately or by the choices we have made over the years—and there may have been several changes in one's career direction and ways of thinking. Now is the time to take stock of life and to ponder some important questions. *What have I accomplished? Where have I been going? What do I believe? What changes will I make as I move into my thirties?*

Some people have no difficulty answering these questions. Their lives tend to be complete and satisfactory. Settled into careers, growing as family members, and aware of their goals and beliefs, these people have moved through their twenties, have found their place as adults, and feel free to grow without making major changes.

As you might guess, for most people the late twenties are more stressful. It is common to be dissatisfied with life thus far and to feel uncertainty about how to plan for the future. Sometimes there is more severe worry and floundering as people experience what has been called the "age thirty crisis."[5] This is a time of turmoil in those who realize that the apprentice years for adulthood are nearing an end. If they haven't done so already, now is the time to "settle down," to get established at some place in the society, and to get on with the business of serving the Lord and building a family and/or career.

It is difficult to flounder at any age, but perhaps it is harder to be goalless when you are about to turn thirty. Many of your friends may seem to have found a direction in life, and some people, including your parents, may be critical or impatient with you if you haven't "settled down." As you get older, you know it may be more difficult to launch a career or a marriage. You probably have broader experience and a more realistic perspective than most twenty-year-olds, and you know that it would be highly inaccurate for you to assume that all is hopeless. Nevertheless, the approach of age thirty gives many people a nudge to take a serious look at life and to make whatever changes seem wise.

Setting Life Patterns

In a highly popular book that once topped the bestseller list, Gail Sheehy suggested that people develop "life patterns" while they are in their twenties.[6] Because we have only one life, each choice that we make and each goal that we pursue means that there are a number of other things that we cannot do. By the time we reach thirty it is becoming clear how these earlier choices have sent our lives in a direction and created "patterns" that can now be seen.

Apparently Sheehy doesn't have any scientific basis for this theory; it is built mostly on her observations and interviews. It would be wrong to assume that these patterns are rigid or unchangeable, and Sheehy herself is careful to emphasize that since people are unique, many individuals don't fit any of these patterns. Having said this, it still could be interesting to ponder how patterns may have been developing in your life.

Looking first at men, Sheehy noticed three prominent patterns. The *transients* are people who have been unwilling or unable to make any firm commitment during their twenties. For as long as possible, they try to stay young and resist facing adult responsibilities.

I once knew a student like this. He worked in a church as a youth worker until he was thirty. He had no vocational or financial goals, few friends his own age, few possessions except for a sports car, a very poor self-concept, and an unstable marriage to a girl who was much like him. Eventually, he "grew up" and started to build a more stable life, but not until his marriage collapsed, his youth work faltered, he took an honest look at himself as he approached thirty, and he concluded that life changes could only be made by him and with God's help.

In contrast, *locked in* people make solid commitments in their twenties and are able to avoid the struggles and crises that other young men face. People who enter a family business without giving this much thought, or those who find a job and stay there without much self-examination, may feel secure in life but some of these people may also feel stifled. They do what is expected, take few risks, and often reach mid-life only to discover that they are bored, angry, in a rut, and frustrated because they never took the time, during their twenties, to explore the world of work or to look carefully at themselves.

Less common, but sometimes more noticed are the *wunderkind* men who are workaholics, hard-driving, goal-dominated, ambitious, and seemingly filled with energy. Most are also insecure, afraid to let down their guard, insensitive, and vaguely hoping that their insecurities will vanish when they reach the top.

I am reluctant to admit that this description once fit me until I began to see, with God's help and my wife's gentle prodding, that my genuinely productive life wasn't as fulfilling as I believed. In reality it was empty and frantic. I had to work at becoming what has since been called an *integrator*.

The integrator is the man who tries to balance his ambitions with a genuine commitment to his family and a desire to combine "economic comfort with being ethical and beneficial to society." In what must be a classic understatement, Sheehy notes that "this is obviously not an easy pattern to follow."[7] It is a life pattern that rarely is attained before the mid-thirties, and it never comes unless one decides to work for it. Such a life pattern, it seems, is the one most consistent with biblical standards for living.

There are other male patterns. These include *never-married men* who are a minority in our society and who may or may not be well adjusted, *latency boys* who remain bound to their mothers throughout adult life, and *paranurturers* who devote themselves not to building careers, but to serving others. Many missionaries, medical practitioners, and clergymen are paranurturers. Their dedication and achievements are often admirable, especially if they are realistic enough to take care of their own needs as well as the needs of others.

Some of the patterns that describe men, could also be applied to women. Transient and never-married women, for example, are assumed to be similar to their male counterparts. In addition, Sheehy suggests some uniquely female life patterns.

The *caregiver* usually marries in her twenties and has little intention of going beyond the domestic role. Most are strongly behind their husbands' careers, and although some may work outside the home their major dedication is to the family. It is there that they find genuine satisfaction as a homemaker and helpmeet.

In time, however, caregivers can begin to feel locked in to this role, taken for granted, and unable to be personally fulfilled or genuinely creative. If her whole life has been centered on the home, there can be great difficulty when a husband's death or departure, financial crisis, or a family breakup forces the woman to fend for herself in a sink-or-swim way. Some modern writers would suggest that women should protect themselves from all of this by never getting into the caregiving role in the first place. Such an attitude tends to deny that there can be meaning and fulfillment as a homemaker. At some point, however, "every caregiver must learn to care a little more for herself,"[8] and to develop some of her own interests. The earlier this is done, the less are problems likely to be encountered later in life.

Early in adulthood, some women develop an *either-or* life pattern. In their twenties these people feel they must choose between either love and children or work and accomplishment. In making this decision, the young woman may hope to have both a family and a career eventually, but she decides to pursue one of the alternatives first and to defer the other until later. With many women this seems to work, but there is often a lot of frustration involved, especially when it comes time to change direction in later life. Sheehy has made the perceptive observation that if men were presented with a similar choice. there might not be any husbands.[9]

Wouldn't it be better for the young woman to develop an *in-*

tegrator life pattern similar to that of men? In theory this sounds good: work to be a good mother, wife, homemaker, and career builder all at the same time. Gail Sheehy took that road herself, but reached an interesting and disturbing conclusion. "It rarely is possible for a woman to integrate marriage, career, and motherhood in her twenties and it's about time some of us who have tried said so. It is quite possible to do so at 30 and decidedly possible at 35, but before then, the personal integration necessary . . . simply hasn't had a chance to develop."[10] If you try to do everything in your twenties, you will wear out quickly and in time something will have to be given up—one's career, one's family, one's marriage, or one's sanity (she means that seriously and not as a joke).

In earlier eras many women were locked in to female roles and had little opportunity to develop personally or professionally. Then the liberation movement raised some legitimate questions about women's rights but, at least in some segments, implied that real women were those who shunned traditional roles and competed with men in building careers. Is it possible, however, for people of both sexes to be both nurturers and achievers without running themselves ragged? Can we keep both options open, focus our primary attention on one, but keep the other from dying?

The young woman, for example, may decide to start career building, but without ignoring the importance of nurturing. If there are no children to care for, she could teach a Sunday school class or find some other ways to nurture. When there are children in the house, the wife and her husband should be sure that the mother has time and opportunity to develop career skills and abilities. This boosts the woman's self-concept and keeps her ready to take a more active role in a career world later.

The Christian husband should not resist this balance. Read

Proverbs 31 to see how the woman of noble character did not necessarily have to stay at home all day. Ephesians 5:25, 28 and similar New Testament passages show that the husband has a major responsibility to nurture the family, even if he is involved in career building. Perhaps it *is* true that both males and females will have to shed some traditional roles if we are to find balanced and integrated life patterns.

Moving and Taking Root

The emerging of life patterns is sometimes complicated by the fact that we live in a very mobile society. Travel is relatively easy and inexpensive. Large companies and the military move their employees frequently and, as we saw in an earlier chapter, sometimes disrupt whole families in the process. When we are young this may be easy and sometimes exciting, but the older we get, the harder it is to move.

Many young people are now finding that it is also hard to stay in one location, trying to acquire a home.[11] Home ownership used to be part of the American dream and a possibility for almost anyone who worked hard and could save enough for a down payment. But then prices started to skyrocket. Interest rates and inflation both went up, and the prospects of owning a home grew dim for many young couples. Owning a home is no longer a mark of success or stability. For many it isn't much more than a not-too-realistic hope. If you doubt this, visit your local real estate office.

Are there ways out of the housing dilemma, other than renting for life? According to some experts, the answer is yes. Parents can sometimes help with a down payment that a young person can pay back in small amounts over time. Others have discovered that condominiums or mobile homes can be a place to start—and as a fringe benefit there may be little or no worry about mowing big lawns or shoveling snow. Some people have recognized that houses are cheaper the further one is from the city. To buy a house in the country and make a long commute can be tiring for a while, but for many people, this may be the best route to later home ownership in a more convenient location.

In considering this, it is also important to look at one's values. Is it important for you to own a home? Is it important to be in a convenient location? Have you learned how to manage money (see table 9-1)? Are you willing to make the necessary sacrifices to pay the mortgage, utility bills, maintenance costs, and taxes? If you are one of the many people who would answer yes, try to avoid the all-too-common problem of buying way beyond your means. It is possible that the home you own, could begin to own and control you. A reliable real estate agent and your local banker can often give guidance as you ponder these issues. Remember, too, that the God who will supply our needs (including shelter) can guide as you make decisions about housing.

It has been said that in our society you aren't really an adult until you have a mortgage. I don't think this is true, but there are few things that can confront you with the realities of adult living like the realization that you have agreed to make house payments for the next thirty years.

Settling Into Communities

Home ownership, and to a lesser extent home rental, forces us to face the fact that we live in communities. We are members of a family and sometimes of a church, part of a company or student body, residents of an apartment complex, neighborhood, or rural county. As we get older we see more clearly how life can be influenced by television, political parties, government decisions, the Internal Revenue Service, local banks and merchants, the police department, the courts, unions, employers, schools, drunken drivers, lawbreakers, the whims and life-styles of our neighbors, and the activities of volunteer groups and self-help organizations. Each of these, and a host of other community influences, involves people. We might try to ignore their ideas and actions but we are affected nevertheless.

We are also able to participate in many community activities. Carl Jung, the Swiss psychoanalyst, argued that young adults are so busy getting their careers and families established that they rarely have time for active community involvement until they are approaching forty. It probably is more true that individual interests and personality traits lead some people to be heavily involved in community issues while others prefer to remain apart, regardless of age.

It has been suggested that within a church, a college, a community, a political party, a union, or any other social group (including a family), individuals tend to take one of six possible positions.[12] As you read the following paragraphs, you might want to ponder where you fit. Probably the extent of your involvement will depend on the group. It is unlikely, for example, that you will have an equal degree of involvement in your church, your profession, your neighborhood, or local politics. And as you grow older, the extent of your involvement in each of these areas of life might change.

One way to participate in a group is to be a *detractor,* who tries to impede the work that others are doing. This is the person who refuses to cooperate, sometimes disobeys laws, is highly critical, and actively tries to disrupt the group's work and activities. Hardened criminals are in this category, but so may be gossips or honest people who sincerely believe that a group or community activity needs to be stopped.

In contrast, the *mere member* pays little or no attention to what is happening. He or she obeys the law and pays taxes, but there is little attempt to be informed on issues and not much inclination to vote or get involved—except for occasional griping.

The *observer* knows what is going on in politics, the government, the world, the church, the city hall, the local business, or even the family. This person may be well informed and able to discuss issues intelligently, but there is no inclination to get involved or try to bring changes.

As you can guess, the *participant* is different. He or she is both informed and at least minimally active. This is the person who will sign petitions, make the effort to vote, attend an occasional business or political meeting, and sometimes give a minor contribution.

More active is the *contributor*. This person is informed, a willing worker, and one who votes, expresses opinions, and often contributes financially without even being asked to do so. It should not be assumed that the contributor is always wealthy or middle-aged. Many young adults take an active and highly significant role in political and other community issues, although they sometimes are frustrated by older people who resist new ideas and youthful involvement.

The *leader,* as you might expect, is deeply involved. Politics, the church, government service, or community issues may be this person's major interest. Sometimes the involvement is self-serving—a way to get power, prestige, or other payoffs—but this isn't always true. There are people, including young adults, who sincerely are concerned about community issues and want to do what they can to change things for the better.

Where do you fit in all of this? You might take one of these six positions in terms of your church, another in terms of local politics or the PTA, and still another in terms of a union or professional organization. In a free society, you are better able to choose the extent of your involvement, and as you get older you might find that your attitudes and participation will both change.

There is some evidence that as people get older they also become less naive and more inclined to be cynical. The naive tend to be overly optimistic and ill informed. The cynical person often feels powerless, critical, and smugly arrogant. If you hope to make any kind of positive impact on society, it would seem that you must go between the extremes of naiveté and cynicism, to reach a stage of realistic optimism. Here is the belief that in spite of all the problems, things can get better if people are willing to work for improvements.

Jesus had this attitude. He knew, for example, that there always would be poor people, but this didn't stop Him from meeting their needs and encouraging others to do the same. Jesus was concerned about preparing people for a kingdom that is not of this world, but He knew about local politics and spoke out on occasion, and He was deeply involved in social as well as spiritual issues. If we claim to be His followers, what does that say about our involvement with others?

Looking Ahead to Middle Age

Do you remember the Old Testament account of the life of Jacob?[13] He was a schemer who didn't get along with his brother and eventually had to leave home to save his life. In those days it wasn't easy to travel, of course, and at one point in the journey to the home of his uncle, Jacob stopped for the night and slept on the ground. The dream that Jacob had that night was recorded in the Bible and has been described in Sunday school classes ever since.

Jacob saw a ladder resting on earth and with its top in heaven. Angels were ascending and descending the ladder and at the top stood God. He gave His blessing to Jacob and promised to be with him and to watch over him.

It isn't surprising that Jacob was deeply moved. He built an altar to worship God, promised to serve Him, and vowed to give the Lord a tenth of all future income. At this time in his life, Jacob was probably a young adult.

I thought of this incident when I first read the Yale research about people who have reached the age thirty transition. During the twenties they have been getting established in terms of values, careers, and family. Now they are full-fledged adults and they are faced with the two major challenges of the thirties: establishing a niche in the society and working to advance toward one's goals.[14]

The best way to think of this time in life, say the Yale researchers, is to use the picture of a ladder. By the time a person reaches his or her early thirties, life patterns have been formed and a foundation for adulthood has been laid. In front of us stands a ladder with rungs taking us to career success, fame, power, stability, achievement, and perhaps even happiness. For some people the goals at the top of the ladder are clear; for others the top rungs may still be vague and in the clouds. For almost everyone, there is a sense of hope. The young adult, now a junior member of the society, starts to climb toward becoming a respected senior member of society.

Many will slip during this climb and some will fall. Others will go up a rung or two and either give up or find that some obstacle—perhaps the prejudice of others, lack of opportunity, insufficient education, health failure, discouragement, or lack of motivation—prevents them from going any farther.

Jacob kept going, in spite of frustrations, mistakes, and the deception of his uncle. Life success and personal happiness undoubtedly were important to Jacob, but these were not at the top of his ladder. God stood there and Jacob went through adulthood believing in the Lord's promises. At least once, he wrestled with God and there may have been times when Jacob wondered if he had been forgotten. But God, as always, was faithful. Jacob, whose name was changed to Israel, became the father both of God's people throughout the centuries and of a modern nation.[15]

As you move through young adulthood and on into your thirties and beyond, what will become of you? At this point nobody knows, but some concluding comments might be worth pondering.

Pondering Some Conclusions

It is impossible to estimate how many self-help books have appeared, especially in the United States and Canada, during the past couple of decades. Many of these books are like this one, written to give information, to raise warnings, and to help readers cope with the challenges of life. It may surprise you to know that there is almost no research on the value and limitations of self-help books or articles. Nobody knows, for sure, whether this or any other book will be helpful.

What we do know is that God meets our needs and will guide those who are willing to let Him lead.[16] Jacob committed his life to God and experienced divine guidance, even though life continued to be stressful. In the midst of our modern stresses, you and I can trust Him too. And it is possible that, in His goodness, He will have used the words in this book to help both reader and author live lives that are more pleasing to Him.

The pursuit of happiness that de Tocqueville saw many years ago, has been expanded in our more modern times.[17] We now seem to believe that life can be free of stress; that all of us can be self-sufficient and capable of coping with every situation; that the right mental attitude can get us anything we want; that personal fulfillment and self-actualization are the most important goals in life; that to be normal and healthy we must be free of problems, struggles, and worries; and (this concerns me the most) that psychology is so powerful it can solve all our problems.

Each of these conclusions can be challenged. I believe that each is wrong. Of course we can learn to cope with stress, work to change our mental attitudes, strive toward our life goals, develop skills for living, and get help from psychology. If I didn't believe this, I would not have written this book.

But life isn't easy and neither is it problem-free. It isn't easy to be a young adult, or an older one either. God never promised that we would have heaven on earth in our lifetime. Some of the problems and struggles that hurt us the most are also the greatest opportunities for growth. We can't always take these away, even with all of our determination, mental attitudes, and modern technology. Such words are not written to squelch your optimism. They are written, instead, to suggest that you can have a realistic perspective on life; a perspective that is characterized by hope.

The unnamed writer of Psalm 71 must have been getting to the end of adulthood when the following words were written.

> Lord, you are my refuge! Don't let me down! . . . O Lord, you alone are my hope; I've trusted you from childhood. Yes, you have been with me from birth and have helped me constantly—no wonder I am always praising you! My success—at which so many stand amazed—is because you are my mighty protector. All day long I'll praise and honor you, O God, for all that you have done for me. And now, in my old age, don't set me aside. Don't forsake me now when my strength is failing. . . . I will keep on expecting you to help me. I praise you more and more.[18]

Here is somebody who had gone through life, knowing that there would be problems and challenges, but expecting God to guide. That is a theme that goes through the whole Bible. A later example comes from the New Testament Book of 2 Peter.

This little three-chapter epistle was written when times were difficult, immorality was rampant, and even the church was infiltrated with people who called themselves believers but who were slaves to their own self-centered lusts, ambition, and heresy. The readers were warned to resist godless values and encouraged to remember that Christ would at some time return to this earth. Then, as the Book draws to a close, there are several concise statements that can apply to modern readers, including young adults.

"Live holy and godly lives." That isn't a very popular message today and it certainly isn't an easy requirement, but it is at the core of Christian teaching. By our own efforts, it is impossible to live holy lives, especially in modern society, but with God's help we can "make every effort to be found spotless, blameless and at peace with him."[19]

Then, we are encouraged to be "on our guard." It is easy to fall into thinking that the Lord has forgotten us, that society's values are really right, that our Christian faith is irrelevant, or that error is really truth. The way to avoid such error is to make a practice of pondering and recalling "the words spoken in the past by the holy prophets and the command given by our Lord and Savior" through the writers of Scripture.[20]

Then we must learn to "grow in the grace and knowledge of our Lord and Savior Jesus Christ."[21] Growth doesn't come because we want it. Physical growth comes when we eat and exercise our bodies. In the spiritual realm it is no different. When we "feast" on the Word of God and take the time to know God, we begin to grow.

Commenting on this whole epistle, one writer has written a sentence that is worth reading more than once. "The fact is that faith without knowledge degenerates into pietism; purely emotional religion leads, often enough, to immorality, which militates against stability as almost nothing else does."[22]

Surely this is the best self-help formula that anyone can have for living this life: A faith in Christ that is strengthened by a consistent reading of the Scripture and by increasing knowledge of Christ.

This is also the basis of a happiness that is much more lasting than what de Tocqueville described. All of us know that life is never problem-free. Without stresses much of life's challenge would be gone and our time on this earth would be bland and boring. But Christ has come to make life abundant, at every age in life.

As part of a seminar on young adulthood, somebody wrote the following words on a tiny slip of paper. "As I move through young adulthood, I am coming to realize that the Lord only gives us a certain span of time to live. I want to use my life for a good purpose: to be able to face my Lord and hear Him say 'well done, good and faithful servant.' "

That is a fitting goal for anyone.

Table 9-1
Handling Finances

Long before we reach adulthood, most of us recognize that it isn't easy to handle money. Bills seem to accumulate a lot faster than income, and the easy availability of credit plunges many young people (and older people as well) into debt that adds to the financial burden.

Numerous books and articles have been written on money management. Your local library or bookstore probably has several that you might want to read. The following are some general principles that others have found to be helpful.

1. Recognize that good money management involves a desire to manage money well, skills in knowing how to manage money, and a clear idea of one's values (what we consider important in life).

2. The Bible says a lot about money and possessions. Read the following passages and ask how they apply to you: Matthew 6:19–34; Deuteronomy 15:7–11; 1 Timothy 6:6–10, 17–19; James 2:1–7; 1 John 3:17, 18; Philippians 4:12, 19. When you have read these, ponder the message in each of the following: Amos 5:11–15; 1 Kings 3:3–14; Matthew 19:16–30; Luke 21:1–4; Acts 2:44, 45, 4:11, 32–35.

3. Ask God to help you with your finances. Realize that books and articles can arouse guilt in readers. How you manage your money is between you and God.

4. Recognize that there is nothing wrong with money or possessions; what is wrong is the love of money and the drive to accumulate possessions. God can help you to change such attitudes.

5. It has been said that the amount of money you have is less important than the way in which your money is managed. Consider the following management suggestions:

- When you get your pay, try to put aside some money for savings, and some for God's work. (As a goal, you might try to save 10 percent and give another 10 percent to Christian work. Once you get into the habit of doing this, you will get to the point where you don't miss the money.)
- Try to avoid borrowing or using credit cards, except in extreme emergencies.
- Take some time to set some financial objectives. What things are important for you?
- Rank your financial priorities. What do you want first? What are you willing to wait for?
- Avoid impulse buying—especially if you are being pressured by a salesperson. What is on sale at one time will probably be on sale again. If you are contemplating a major purchase, discuss this with your mate or a friend before proceeding.
- Develop a spending plan. Write down you annual income, make a note of your giving and fixed income (like mortgage and taxes), and then estimate your expenses. Try to set a realistic budget and stick to it.
- Keep accurate records. That is time-consuming, but accurate records not only help at tax time. They let you see where your money is going, how accurate your budget plan has been, and whether there is need for change.

6. Remember that everything we have is from God. He can help us to be good stewards of our money, and to have an attitude of gratefulness and a willingness to share what we have with others.

7. When things get financially difficult, remember that God does supply our needs. See Philippians 4:19; Matthew 21:22; John 16:23, 24.

Source Notes

1. The quotation and summary are taken from Alexis de Tocqueville, *Democracy in America* (New York: Alfred A. Knopf, 1944), vol. 2, pp. 144, 145.

2. Philippians 4:12.

3. This thinking, observed among people in their late twenties, was reported in Daniel J. Levinson et al., *The Seasons of a Man's Life* (New York: Alfred A. Knopf, 1978), pp. 58, 85.

4. Ibid.

5. Ibid.

6. Gail Sheehy, *Passages* (New York: Bantam, 1976), pp. 250–347.

7. Ibid., p. 289.

8. Ibid., p. 311.

9. Ibid., p. 312.

10. Ibid., p. 340.

11. Jerry Edgerton, "The Baby Boomers: A Home of Their Own," *Money*, vol. 12, March 1983, pp. 86–87, 90, 94.

12. R. R. Carkhuff, *How to Help Yourself: The Art of Program Development* (Amherst, Mass.: Human Resources Development Press, 1974).

13. The account of this can be read in Genesis 27 and 28.

14. Levinson, op. cit., pp. 59–60, 140–41.

15. Genesis 32:22–30.

16. Philippians 4:8; Psalms 32:8; Proverbs 3:5, 6.

17. Some of the ideas in this paragraph are adapted from Bernie Zilbergeld, *The Shrinking of America: Myths of Psychological Change* (Boston: Little, Brown, 1983).

18. Psalms 71:1, 5–9, 14 TLB.

19. 2 Peter 3:11, 14.

20. 2 Peter 3:17.

21. 2 Peter 3:18.

22. Michael Green, *The Second Epistle of Peter and the Epistle of Jude* (Grand Rapids: Wm. B. Eerdmans, 1968), p. 150.

Index